THE ENCYCLOPEDIA OF
GOLF

THE ENCYCLOPEDIA OF
GOLF

CHRIS MEADOWS

WITH ALLEN F. RICHARDSON

Bath · New York · Singapore · Hong Kong · Cologne · Delhi · Melbourne

This edition published by Parragon in 2007

Copyright © Parragon Books Ltd 2001

Parragon
Queen Street House
4 Queen Street
Bath BA1 1HE, UK

Produced by terryjeavons&company

ISBN 978-1-4054-7351-4

Printed in China

Photography by Bill Johnston
Course illustrations by Rod Ferring

Film kindly supplied by Fuji

ACKNOWLEDGMENTS

I would like to thank The Wisley Golf Club, Surrey, England and Le Prince de Provence, Vidauban, France for allowing me the use of their wonderful golfing facilities. They are truly two of the finest golf courses to be found anywhere in Europe.

Thanks also go to my professional colleague Daniel Belcher, Nicola Bustin, my wife Kayo, to the two men who worked so closely with me in over a year of preparation, Allen F. Richardson and Bill Johnston, but most of all to my teacher Ian Connelly who developed my love for golf and gave me the passion to teach this great game.

The publishers would like to thank the following for use of images:

Getty Images: pp108/9, pp198/9, p200, p203, p205, p208, p209, p210, p213, p214, p217 and p219.

Phil Sheldon Golf Picture Library: p207.

CONTENTS

ABOUT THE AUTHOR

Chris Meadows' passion for teaching the game was inspired and fostered by Scottish professional, Ian Conelly. Over an eight-year period working with him as pupil and teacher, Meadows vowed to develop his own school of excellence. In 1987 he acquired the Regent's Park Golf & Tennis School in London, which became an outstanding success, and in 1997 he opened the first Metro Golf Centre in London. These incorporate everything a golfer might ever need to advance their game. As a golf teaching professional, Meadows has spread his message through instructional columns, half a dozen books, television (from BBC and Channel 4 to satellite), instructional videos and interactive websites.

INTRODUCTION

Golfers are dreamers and seekers.

From the first time we pick up a club and hit that small, round object known as a golf ball towards the sky, we are part of a tradition that stretches back through generations of time, linking us to an ancient shepherd who first struck a rock with a stick along the coastal grassland of Scotland.

From that moment we often embark on a life-long quest to improve how we play the game – a game that for most of us eventually becomes both a love and an obsession. From tour pro to club champion to rank beginner, we constantly tinker with our swings, adjust our grips and stances, and try to plant an endless series of 'swing thoughts' in our brains.

The hope is that by tomorrow, next weekend – or at least the end of the year – we will finally play a miracle round.

Golfing dreams

The form that round takes will vary. We might dream of breaking 100 or 70, sinking an eagle putt, winning the club championship, or standing on the 18th tee with a chance to seize the Open. But at the very least,

we all yearn for the day when we'll win that side bet struck with our similarly devoted friends, while savouring a drink at the 19th hole. Then we'll enjoy the afterglow of a memorable day, with everyone mentally replaying their rounds, and generously reviewing each other's remembered highlights.

But even when we are not playing the game, we take lessons, analyze how more gifted players perform on television and read countless articles about the latest technology in club design, swing theory and putting technique.

I know. I've spent a lifetime playing, teaching and trying to improve my own game – and this book is the product of my quest, while your purchase of it is undoubtedly proof that you share my passion.

But now it's time to simplify things.

RIGHT The hours spent working on my game have been some of the most enjoyable of my life. I hope this book also makes learning fun for you in your quest to improve your game.

The Encyclopedia of Golf is structured around a single, essential idea: instead of worrying about all the things you think you need to know, this book will allow you to focus on the essentials that you simply cannot do without.

One small step

They say that the journey of a lifetime starts with one step. So try my path, at least for a time. No matter what your standard of play is at the moment, I believe I can quickly take you to your current goal, and then beyond.

In order to do that, this book is structured so that anyone – from a complete beginner to an advanced player – can either dip into it for specific advice, or simply enjoy reading it from cover to cover. I've started with the basics of what equipment you need to play the game, then take you through how to assume a proper grip, stance and posture, the importance of a pre-shot routine, the mechanics of how to develop and perfect your own 'repeatable'

swing – plus everything you need to know about the short game around the greens, which can account for some 50 per cent of your strokes in any given round.

Secrets of the pros

Beyond that, there are chapters on more sophisticated techniques. I reveal pros' secrets about how to get out of trouble spots such as the rough, water and sand. I teach you how to hit a variety of speciality shots, often dictated by the course and conditions. I also help you to develop a course strategy that lets you play the game within your personal limits.

Ten of the best courses in the world are featured, to tempt you to greater things, and there are some tips about the complex rules of golf that can ultimately save you strokes. But perhaps best of all, I'll show you how to cure the many problems that can (and do) creep into anyone's game – including my own.

Take on board this knowledge, and you'll be ready to meet the the challenges of this game at any time in the future, because golf really is a game for life.

ABOVE The great thing about golf is that we are always learning. When, as human beings, we have mastered the wildest dreams of future technology, we will still be working on our golf swings!

ABOVE LEFT Over the years I have had the opportunity to work with some great teachers who have shared their knowledge with me. It is now my privilege to share my knowledge with you.

1 EQUIPMENT

Purchasing golf equipment is like choosing a pair of shoes for a child. If they do not fit correctly, they will be uncomfortable and have undesirable long-term consequences.

CHOOSING A PUTTER

Putting is the most individual aspect of the game and golfers approach this shot with a variety of pre-shot routines, set-ups and grips. Not surprisingly, the club they use varies enormously.

ABOVE There is an enormous variety of putters. Soft face, titanium face, Ping, Zing, Wild Thing – the list is endless. But before you buy, just ask one question – do I believe I can get the ball in the hole with this?

RIGHT Putters are often marked on the grip with their length.

Putters can have shafts that are extremely short or as long as a broomstick handle. The blade can be flat on both sides of the head, partially rounded on one side like a mallet, heel-shafted, centre-shafted or offset. Some sport a flange, and many have an aiming line – or even two – to assist in sizing up the target.

The shortest club

A few things are constant about putters and how a golfer can use them. The putt is the only shot in golf where the ball does not travel at least partially through the air. The idea is to roll the ball over the short grass on the greens, although in some circumstances you might also putt through the longer grass on the fringe of a green, from parts of the fairway, or even across the sand in a bunker.

But because the ball remains in contact with whatever surface you are trying to cover, the putter is designed as the shortest club in the bag (with the exception of the long-shafted varieties favoured by a minority of players), the most upright, and the one with the least loft – between two and four degrees.

The head is small, and thus meant only for relatively short distances, and the grip – although sometimes round like any other club – is often flat at the front, to accommodate the unique way a golfer holds this club.

Putter characteristics

Putters come with three types of clubhead positions in relation to the shaft: straight, offset and onset. A straight-headed putter face will be level with your hands when you line up. With an offset putter, your hands will be in front of the clubface, while with an onset putter your hands will be behind.

Try all three types of putter to see which one you find easiest to aim. Obviously, taking the right aim is the most important way to sink putts consistently.

Many putters also have lines on the clubhead to help you aim accurately. These line markings should be set precisely at rightangles to the face. Some are also intended to reveal the putter's sweet spot, which can be a tremendous help to the average golfer.

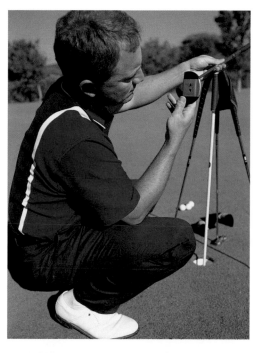

LEFT When you've sampled some putters, you will develop a favourite. Now it's down to good technique and reading the line of the putts.

PRO TIP

Just like any other club in your bag, a putter also has a lie angle, and having the correct one for you is vital to playing successfully on the greens. Choose a lie angle that sets your eyes over the ball when you adopt your posture. That's the secret to aiming correctly.

LEFT The lie angle of a putter is also important. The head of the putter should sit flat on the ground.

BELOW As with other clubs, try a variety of putters on a green before making any decision.

Be careful when considering bargain basement putters. I have come across several models where the markings were less than accurate, and that flaw could affect how many putts you make. Anything that interferes with successful putting is a huge detriment to your game, since nearly half your strokes will be taken on the green.

Balance and swingweight

A putter with good balance and the proper swingweight for you is vital to executing a smooth putting stroke. The term balance refers to the distribution of weight in the clubhead, while swingweight is the weight distribution along the length of the whole club.

You may have heard the term 'heel and toe', which refers to the most popular form of balance in putters. With a heel-and-toe putter, most of the weight is concentrated in the two ends of the blade. The idea is to prevent the putter from twisting in your hands when the blade strikes the ball. If it does, the ball will go off line.

The swingweight of putters can vary from very light to quite heavy. Many good golfers prefer a heavier club, which helps them to make a smooth, rhythmic motion.

THE GOLF BALL

After clubs, manufacturers spend most money marketing and advertising golf balls, promising that each new model is vastly improved and guaranteed to fly straighter, run further or – paradoxically – land softer, with the sort of spin you see the great professionals achieving.

The truth is, a golf ball alone cannot guarantee that dream round. But the right ball for you can certainly help your game, while the wrong one can definitely damage it. With a myriad of choices at the average pro shop or golf store, how do you choose the right one?

Colour and performance

Let's make things easy. Colour has nothing to do with performance. Simply choose the colour you like best and proceed from there (a yellow ball is the easiest to spot in murky conditions).

Otherwise, it's what's inside – and to a lesser extent what's outside – a golf ball that really counts. Golf balls are made of one, two or three pieces.

One-piece balls, constructed of a tough, rubberized plastic, are most often used at driving ranges because they can withstand most of the punishment dished out by beginners. They are the cheapest to buy and a good option for new golfers, but they don't fly as far nor as true as more expensive balls.

The majority of golfers find that two-piece golf balls are the best for their game. The cover of a two-piece ball is usually made of surlyn – an extremely tough and long-lasting material – and the inside is filled with various resins which expand and propel the ball forward when hit.

Most manufacturers of two-piece balls emphasize the endurance and extra distance these balls can achieve with a good strike, which is an advantage over both the one-piece and three-piece balls. The downside is that two-piece balls lack the exquisite control of a three-piece ball – the type favoured by most tour professionals. Most golfers opt for endurance and distance.

Spin and feel

Only single-figure handicap players and pros strike the ball consistently enough to get the full advantage of the more expensive three-piece ball, which has a liquid centre surrounded by wound fibres, and a cover of either surlyn or balata.

Balata is thin and soft, which gives the greatest feel and spin, but is also easily cut by the slightest mishit. As a result, even pros must replace their ball every few holes. Some choose to replace them on every hole if they consistently hit hard down on the ball.

Finally, when choosing a golf ball, consider its compression factor, which is usually stated on the side of the box as '80', '90' or '100'. The 90 is best for the majority of golfers, although women and seniors might wish to experiment with the lower-compression 80s. The 90 performs well in less than ideal temperatures and weather conditions. The 100 is suited to pros and low handicappers, especially for play on warm days.

BELOW LEFT A logo on a ball can make it easier to identify. Otherwise, make a mark on your ball with a felt-tipped pen.

BELOW RIGHT If you want distance, choose a two-piece ball with a surlyn cover.

THE GOLF SHOE

The average round involves several hours of walking over often awkward terrain in unpredictable weather. The correct golf shoe not only offers comfort and support, but also provides the very foundation of the game – the anchor for a golfer's swing.

The correct set-up and stance depends on a secure footing, and a successful swing demands balance throughout. Golf shoes are built with metal or hard rubber spikes to provide grip and prevent sideways movement of the feet. When the ground is wet and slippery, that becomes doubly important.

Choosing a shoe

Most golf clubs have strict rules about footwear. Without a proper pair of shoes – and the right type of spikes – you might not be allowed to play in the first place. So how do you choose the right shoe?
• Wear thick socks when you try each pair on as your feet will swell while playing.
• Ensure that shoes have cushioned inner soles, good arch support and a padded collar around the back to prevent the sides from digging into your ankles.
• Break your shoes in before playing.

Weather considerations

If you expect to play often in the rain, you might consider one-piece shoes constructed from a synthetic material often guaranteed to keep water out completely. Such shoes are very light and easy to care for, but provide little ventilation and will make your feet perspire in dry and warm weather.

Traditional all-leather shoes are ideal for hot and dry conditions because they allow your feet to breathe. But they are heavier than one-piece shoes – which can affect your balance – and need constant polishing, and occasional waterproofing, to prevent damage and cracks.

A compromise is offered by shoes that have leather uppers – to let the feet breathe – and synthetic soles to keep the water out.

Soft spikes

Many golf clubs have banned metal spikes in order to preserve the greens from the disastrous ruts caused by careless golfers 'skating' their spikes across the grass. In place of metal spikes, golfers are required to put soft, plastic studs into their shoes, or to purchase new shoes with rubber-studded soles. Always check ahead to see what the policy is if playing somewhere new.

With soft spikes in your shoes or on rubber-studded soles, you might feel more comfortable on dry, hard ground. There is also the advantage that you can wear your shoes indoors.

ABOVE Many courses these days insist on soft spikes as they are kinder to putting surfaces. If metal spikes are allowed at your course, they are better for winter conditions when it's slippery. Always check the regulations at the course you're playing.

LEFT When buying a new pair of shoes, remove all the spikes before you first play in them and grease each thread (Vaseline is ideal). This will make replacing spikes easier in the future.

2 PREPARATION

A golf swing takes around one second to perform. Therefore, the position you assume at the set-up is critical – it will either enable or disable your golf swing from the word 'go'.

GOLF'S FUNDAMENTALS

At one time it was fashionable to think of golfers as anything but athletic. After all, golf – even at the highest level – is played at a leisurely pace by men and women of all ages, and, in some cases, by children. Endurance is hardly a necessity, and no running, jumping or heavy lifting is required.

In fact, it seemed that to play the game in a mere three to four hours, all one had to do was walk a few miles – or in some cases, not even that. Many courses (especially in America) provide – or even require – golfers to use a motorized cart or have a caddie to carry one's bag.

But watching a slow-motion video of golfers through the ages, from the legendary Ben Hogan to current superstars such as Tiger Woods, proves conclusively otherwise. Swinging a golf club in the correct way involves a series of finely tuned and very athletic moves, none of which is possible without the right set-up.

Perfecting such fundamentals as the correct stance, posture and grip makes all the difference once a golfer finally lets it rip, leading either to a pure, clean hit – or any number of golfing disasters. Spending time getting the fundamentals right is one of the soundest golfing investments you can make.

The grip

Most golfers think that the grip is one of the least glamorous aspects of the golf swing. But assuming the proper grip can be a thing of beauty – look at how athletic and powerful the grips of many professionals appear next time you watch a golf tournament. And forming a proper grip is certainly the essential starting point to playing that dream round.

Think of it this way. If the clubhead is the only object that comes into direct contact with the ball, the grip is the only part of a golfer's anatomy that makes contact with the club. In other words, a golfer uses the grip to transfer any power and skill he or she might possess to the object that propels the ball towards the hole.

GRIPPING THE CLUB

Once you've aimed the clubhead, apply the hands to the club. For the right hander, always begin with your left hand followed by the right.

Begin by placing the club across the middle joint of the index finger of your left hand and under the palm pad of your hand. The left hand thumb should fall sightly right of centre on the club. Ensure the back of your left hand and the palm of your right hand point at the target.

Forming a proper grip

Here's how to assume a correct grip.

It has often been said that no two grips – like individual swings – are exactly alike. However, there are certain basics. Once you understand and master those, you can adjust and experiment with your grip until it is comfortable and suits your swing.

But first a quick word of warning here. Forming the proper grip can take weeks, if not months, of practice before doing so becomes second nature. The golf grip is not a particularly natural positioning of the hands.

So dedicated golfers might like to keep a club handy and practise taking their grip while watching television or during a break at work. And if you are in the process of changing your grip, avoid hitting golf shots for as long as it takes to become comfortable with that change.

Positioning the left hand

Allow your arms to hang naturally by your sides and then rest the sole of a club on the ground. Now place the grip of the club in the left hand leaving the top half-inch (1.3cm) of the club protruding from the top of your hand.

Position the club so that it runs diagonally from the middle joint of your index finger to the bottom joint of your little finger, then rest the club against the fleshy pad at the bottom of your hand. Finally, wrap your fingers around, with your thumb falling slightly to the right of centre down the shaft.

Now take a look at what you've done. You should be able to see two knuckles on the back of your hand, and a V – formed by the line between the first joint of the index finger and the thumb – pointing towards your right ear or shoulder.

Now place your right hand on the golf club, positioning your club in the two centre fingers of your hand. It is essential that your club is held in your fingers and not in the palm of your hand. Your little finger should sit in the cleft between the index and middle finger of your left hand.

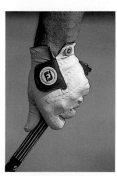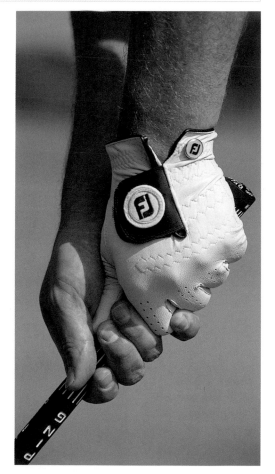

Now close your right hand over your left thumb so that it is covered by your right hand. The thumb and forefinger of your right hand should either touch or almost touch.

THE RIGHT HAND IN THE GRIP

It's time to add the right hand to your grip. A word of caution, especially if you are right-handed: make sure the right hand does not try to take over the grip and dominate your left hand.

The golf grip is different from many other things we do in life with our hands. In the case of the golf grip, both hands must work together, rather than separately. Think of it as shaking hands with yourself, or clapping. You want each hand to be an equal partner, working together.

When the complete grip is assumed, the image of clapping becomes even more appropriate. A good grip requires the palms of each hand to face each other, with the back of the left hand and the palm of the right hand also facing the target.

BELOW The three basic types of grip.

Adding the right hand

The right hand can be joined to the left in the grip in three different ways, depending on the position of the last or little finger. The three basic golf grips are:

• The interlocking grip, where the right little finger is positoned between the first two fingers of the left hand and the left index finger extends over the back of the right hand.

• The traditional overlapping, or Vardon, grip where the little finger sits in the cleft between the index and middle finger of your left hand.

• The ten-finger or baseball grip, where each hand grips the club separately – the base of the right touching the top of the left – but with the fingers independent of each other.

• Most golfers, pro and amateur alike, favour the Vardon grip for both feel and the effortless way it links the hands together as a unit. It can seem strange initially and it takes getting used to for the beginner.

• The interlocking grip, which Jack Nicklaus used, is useful for golfers with smaller hands. The baseball grip is ideal for children and those with weak hands, although former pro Art Wall used it and was famous for hitting holes-in-one.

THE THREE GRIPS

Interlocking grip.

Overlapping grip.

Baseball grip.

THE NATURAL POSITION OF THE HANDS

A good grip will always ensure that the back of your left hand and palm of your right hand face the target.

The final stage

Assuming the final stage of the grip is easy. Essentially, the right hand holds the club shaft in the fingers – never let it ride up into the palm.

First, position the little finger of your right hand in the cleft between your left forefinger and middle finger. Next, wrap the rest of the fingers of your right hand around the club along the bottom joint, folding over your hand by fitting the vertical crease in your palm around the left thumb.

Meanwhile, your right thumb should run diagonally across the top, the tip resting near or lightly against the first finger of your right hand. The V formed between the thumb and forefinger of your right hand should point between the right shoulder and chin.

Grip pressure

One of the most common faults of beginners is applying too much pressure with their hands, squeezing the club in a death grip. They seem to think that the harder they squeeze the club, the harder they will be able to hit the ball. In fact, this is guaranteed to result in a bad shot.

Over the years, golf instructors have searched for the appropriate analogy on how tightly to hold a club. Some have suggested that one should grip a club no tighter than a fountain pen, others no tighter than an open tube of toothpaste, or a small, fragile bird. My recommendation is simply to hold the club naturally: not too tightly and not too loosely.

Firm but supple

Think again about the athleticism of golf. Your grip should be firm enough to ensure that the club does not slip out of your hands, or that your fingers do not come partially off the shaft at the top of the backswing or during the follow-through. But your grip should also be supple enough not to make you tense up, especially through the forearms.

Any tension in the hands, arms and/or shoulders will destroy your ability to swing the club with the sort of fluid grace you see the best golfers use. In other words, you want to exert only the amount of grip pressure that will let you swing like an athlete.

PASSIVE RIGHT SIDE

When placing your right hand on the golf club, ensure that your right shoulder is lower than your left shoulder. This will help establish your head and body in the correct position at the completed set-up.

GRIPPING HONOURS

Harry Vardon did not invent the popular grip that still bears his name. That honour goes to Johnny Laidlay, the British Amateur champion in 1889 and 1891. But because Vardon was the most famous golfer of his time – winning a record six Open Championships from 1896-1914 – golfers everywhere sought to emulate him when he adopted Laidlay's innovation.

THE SET-UP

Positioning the body in relation to the ball and target is known as the set-up, or stance – and the key word here is balance. All athletic movement takes place from a balanced starting position.

BELOW The foundation of a good golf swing begins with the set-up. The time you spend developing good balance and position will make building your golf swing much easier.

Think of a footballer preparing to take a penalty or a cricketer taking his stance at the wicket. The one thing they have in common is that their feet are positioned on the ground in a dynamic way that will allow them to shift their weight from one foot to another and use their body to propel a ball towards their target. Just like the golf swing.

GET IN POSITION TO SWING

Parallel relationships

Any discussion of the set-up starts from the ground up. One of the unique things about golf is that we set up our body parallel to an imaginary line that runs to the target. We usually refer to this as being square to the target.

We can visualize the set-up position along a set of railway tracks, with the golfer parallel to one rail, and the clubhead, ball and target line along the opposite rail. In the distance, both rails converge like lines of perspective at the target.

Any deviation from this parallel relationship can produce a swing fault, resulting in a loss of distance or directional accuracy. We'll cover that in more detail later in this chapter, under the Pre-shot Routine, where we learn how to aim, set up and swing down those imaginary tracks towards a spot on the fairway or the flagstick.

Good body angles

Everything the golfer does in his or her set-up must conform to the goal of taking a stance in direct relation to where the ball will eventually fly – what the famous golf guru David Leadbetter (associated in particular with the success of Nick Faldo, but also with other names such as Ernie Els and Michelle Wie) likes to call setting up good, level body angles. And setting up any body angle starts with the feet.

For decades, golf instructors have debated the position of the feet in relationship to this line. Some, such as Ben Hogan, favoured having the back foot straight, or perpendicular, to the line of flight, and the front foot angled out towards the target by about 20 to 30 degrees. This works for many tour professionals, but it also tends to shorten or restrict the turn of many less experienced golfers.

Natural positioning

I prefer the approach whereby the feet are placed in the most natural, or athletic, position. In other words, both feet should be lined up with that imaginary railway track, but turned out slightly – about 20 to 30 degrees – in relation to one another.

Picture a clock with the ball at noon. Your left foot should point to around 11 o'clock, your right foot to 1 o'clock. This promotes the most balanced and natural position in which to anchor the set-up, giving the stance what Leadbetter calls 'dynamic balance'. Remember, your feet are the only contact with the ground when you swing the golf club. Positioning them correctly is the key to preventing you from swaying off the ball, or even nearly toppling over as you bring the clubhead around your body at over 100mph (160km/h).

Losing your balance means losing it – period!

ALIGNMENT OF THE CLUBHEAD AND BODY

LEFT Begin by positioning the club so that the leading edge is at right angles to the ball-to-target line. Then align your feet, hips and shoulders so that they are positioned parallel to your ball-to-target line. During practice it's a good idea to put two clubs on the ground, as shown, parallel to your ball-to-target line.

POSITION OF FEET

ABOVE Turning your feet out as shown will help you to maintain your balance and assist your follow-through.

BALL POSITION

LEFT A club placed at right angles to the clubs indicating the ball-to-target line will help you to visualize your ball position.

WEIGHT DISTRIBUTION

One key to balance in the set-up is an even distribution of weight between the left and right foot. Unless you are hitting a short pitch or chip, you should not favour either foot in your set-up.

THE BALANCED SET-UP

The width of your stance and where you position the golf ball in relation to your feet are important fundamentals of a proper set-up.

Short iron.

Medium iron.

Long iron.

Wood.

A standard rule of golf is that a golfer should position his or her feet roughly shoulder-width apart. But what many golfers forget – or don't ever realize – is this means shoulder-width as measured from the inside of the heels, rather than the outside of the feet. The width will also vary slightly according to which club is used, from the driver down to the sand wedge.

The shoulder-width rule begins with a standard 5-iron set-up. In this position, two parallel lines drawn from the outside of the shoulders would end at the inside of the heels. Widen the width a few inches for the longer irons and woods, and narrow it for the shorter irons.

The three positions above show how to position your golf ball. Centre for short irons, middle for medium irons and inside of left heel for long irons and woods.

Experiment by placing the ball just inside your left heel for all shots – see what works and stick to it.

Ball position

Where to position the ball has been a time-honoured argument among golf's coaching gurus and top players. For years Jack Nicklaus advocated putting the ball on a line just inside the left heel for all shots, while others have insisted that the distance of the ball from the front foot should be varied according to the length of the club used.

Experiment until you find the method that works best for your game. Start with the ball opposite the instep of your front foot for the driver, then move the ball back by a quarter inch (0.65cm) or so as you use progressively shorter clubs until you get to the wedges, with the ball roughly in the middle of the stance. Or, like Nicklaus, try to hit every club off the left heel.

In later chapters we will consider variations from the normal position, such as when you want to work the ball low under the wind or high over an intervening tree.

Power and control

Now it is time to move from the feet to the body, since keeping the feet in the right place is only part of the story.

The set-up should be natural and athletic. That means balancing the rest of the body frame over the feet in a way that keeps you stable yet ready to perform the complex and athletic movement of the golf swing. This is how you bring power and control to your game, creating a repeating swing that will help you to strike the ball well and consistently, and giving you a swing that will hold up under pressure, the ultimate test of a swing.

In explaining how this works, I like to borrow an image created by another famous golf guru, Jimmy

Ballard, in his book *How to Perfect Your Golf Swing*. Ballard asked his readers to imagine him standing on a platform, holding a large golf bag that weighed a great deal, with someone below ready to catch that load in his hands.

How would the recipient position himself do this?

Brace yourself

As Ballard explained, anyone in such a position would instinctively spread their feet to about shoulder-width and brace themselves. With the feet well grounded, and the body weight spread from the balls of each foot to the heels of each foot, they would also tend to flex their knees – like a boxer ready to receive or deliver a blow.

In addition, the backside would naturally jut out slightly to straighten the spine, keeping the back erect. Meanwhile, the upper arms would be tucked into the sides of the chest to brace the upper torso.

In other words, the larger muscles of the legs, chest and shoulders would be angled and tied in towards the centre of the body like the supports of a bridge, and the person would be ready to catch that imaginary bag.

Agility and strength

I like Ballard's image for what it teaches us about balance, agility and strength. But I want to stress a further point. Later we will add the actual golf swing to our set-up. So for now, don't get hung up on the idea of simply bracing yourself to catch a heavy load someone might be throwing down to you!

The idea is to create a stance that is athletic, but not one that promotes any restriction or rigidity. In order to repeat a golf swing, it needs a firm, but flexible, foundation.

LEFT AND BELOW The width of your stance increases as your club gets longer. As a rule of thumb, with a medium iron the outside of your heels should be at shoulder-width, whereas with a wood, the inside of your heels should be at shoulder-width.

FAR LEFT Turning your body will soon show whether you are balanced, even without a golf club.

LEFT Practise turning to a coiled position and assessing the foundation of your swing.

POWER POSTURE IN THE SET-UP

The correct posture is the final ingredient that will help your set-up support the golf swing. In fact, posture can dictate how well a golfer swings his or her club. Standing too erect inhibits the shoulder turn and the free movement of the arms, while crouching too much forces the arms to lift up, often resulting in poor contact with the ball.

Take a 5-iron, assume a good grip, and hold the club out from the waist at about a 45-degree angle. Stand straight up – while remaining supple and at ease – then bend from the hips – not the waist. As you do, your backside should jut out slightly into a semi-sitting position and your back, or spine, angle should stay straight.

> **MODEL SET-UPS**
>
> Next time you watch the pros on television or on video, study their set-up position, trying to find the golfer closest to you in size. If you are tall, I would recommend focusing on Ernie Els or Nick Faldo, while shorter players would do well to emulate Ian Woosnam or Gary Player.

Swing radius

Finally, flex your knees slightly and ground the club, letting your arms hang naturally from your upper body, with your left arm forming an almost straight line from the top of the shoulder to the clubhead.

This line constitutes the radius of your swing and you must strive to maintain it as a constant throughout the swing, which we will discuss further in chapters to come.

If you have done all of the above correctly, your weight should feel balanced from the balls of your feet to the heels, and overall, you should feel comfortable, centred, and yet dynamically positioned, in what David Leadbetter calls the 'sit-tall' position.

ESTABLISHING GOOD POSTURE

To establish your posture, simply bend forward from your hips keeping your head up. Now sit back and flex your legs slightly at the knee in order to counterbalance the bend forwards. Your weight should end up slightly backwards of centre.

Now your set-up includes the correct posture and you can create the axis from which a powerful and controlled swing can be executed.

Triangle and steeple

One final note on the set-up. With the left arm straight and the right arm also fully extended – but slightly relaxed – you should expect to feel some pressure under the armpits or up around the highest reaches of your chest.

Later, in the chapter on the golf swing, we will explore the concept of the connected swing and see how this triangle – formed by the arms and chest – is tied together and functions in the backswing as you begin your turn.

Ben Hogan, one of the greatest golfers ever to play the game, called this a triangle with the club emerging like the 'spire of a steeple'.

That's not a bad image for something as beautiful as a well executed golf swing.

CONNECTION

ABOVE Your upper arms should feel a light connection with your chest.

POSITION OF WEIGHT

ABOVE With your posture complete, check that your weight is slightly backwards of centre.

CREATE SPACE

When you sit back in your posture you create space for your golf club and achieve good balance.

ABOVE To sense just how your lower body should feel at set-up, throw something heavy up in the air and catch it. You will instinctively flex in the same way as you should at address.

THE PRE-SHOT ROUTINE

It's as easy as 1–2–3, but a set routine will greatly enhance your consistency – and consistency is the key to golf. Having a reliable, repeating swing helps the golfer hit fairways and greens in the regulation number of shots.

BELOW Visualization of just what you want to do with your shot is crucial. Seeing your shot in your mind will tell your body what you want it to do. Only once you have a clear image in your mind should you attempt to play your shot.

But when a shot is less than perfect, being able to get up and down from bunkers and off the fringe of greens is essential. Once on the green, a solid putting stroke is vital to avoiding three-putts – these are all aided by a pre-shot routine.

If you can add all of the above qualities together, you will have a consistent game, which leads to lower scores and winning golf.

So why not incorporate that idea into the very act of stepping up to the ball – whether it's on the tee, fairway, or green, or in the rough or a hazard – before taking each shot and putt? At the very least, you'll

develop a pre-shot routine that helps you to concentrate on the task ahead and to deal with tension. At the very best, you will play better golf.

Consistency

How can I offer such solid assurance? Because with a pre-shot routine, you have already played the shot in your mind, and having done so, you will know which club to select, how to hit it and where.

Watch the pros. If they have one thing in common, it is that their pre-shot routine never varies, from shot to shot, from day to day – and often throughout their entire careers.

Consistency.

I can't say it enough. It's the key to golf. So develop your own pre-shot routine, and give yourself something to fall back on – something you can always rely on. It's the one weapon in your bag that should never vary.

Visualizing the shot

The pre-shot routine is a blend of the physical skills you learned earlier in this chapter – including the proper posture, alignment and set-up or stance – and certain mental skills that will help you hit the ball to your intended target.

The latter concept is called 'visualization', a method of seeing not only where you want the ball to go, but also how you will get it there.

Most beginners find visualization difficult. But that will improve with experience, especially after accumulating a mental gallery of good shots to call upon when confronted by different situations.

Some aspects of golf do get easier with time, and this is one area that is proof of that. You still may not be able to execute the shot perfectly every time, but

you will at least know how to picture a good outcome. That in turn helps give you the confidence to approach each shot correctly.

Confident approach

Obviously positive thinking is a prerequisite here, especially if the shot you are trying to visualize is a tough one – say over a bunker or out of the rough. At the same time, be realistic. It makes no sense conjuring up the image of a miracle strike – even if you have pulled off a few in the past – or a shot you simply are not capable of hitting. Even when visualizing, you should learn to play within yourself.

Mental images

Get into the habit of starting the pre-shot routine as soon as you walk onto the tee or when you reach your ball on the fairway.

First, try to gauge the difficulty of the shot by studying what lies before you on the course and assessing what the conditions are. Then decide on the type of stroke you want to play and how you will shape the flight of the ball.

Finally, see the shot in your mind, from the moment it leaves the clubhead until it reaches the ground – even down to mentally watching it roll up the fairway or towards the pin on the green.

Always be sure where you are aiming – choose your target, which might or might not be the flagstick, depending on conditions.

Place your clubhead down so that the leading edge of the golf club is at right angles to the ball-to-target line.

Then position your feet, hips and shoulders so that they are parallel to your ball-to-target line.

Once your club and body are in line with the ball-to-target line, place your left hand in position.

Now place the right hand on the golf club – remember to lower your right shoulder when doing this.

A closer target can help your alignment. Choose a piece of grass, or a leaf, lying on your ball-to-target line just in front of the golf club.

SIZING UP THE SHOT

A vital aspect of learning how to control your score during a round – otherwise known as managing your game – is always knowing the distance of the shot to be hit, and thus being able to select the correct club to play it.

Before you ever play golf on a course, you should have practised enough on a range to know roughly how far you hit each club, distances which vary considerably from golfer to golfer.

Once you take your game onto the course, always keep an eye open for the distance markers – often bushes, stakes or sprinkler heads that designate the distance to the green. These will enable you to gauge the distance to the target and therefore what club you need to reach it.

Some golfers can estimate distance visually, but I always think that carrying a 'strokesaver' or 'course map' is an essential. If you can't see the markers, or don't have a caddie, this will save you numerous strokes and allow you to hit and think your way around the course, selecting the right club for each situation. Studying the layout of each hole before playing it is just one more way of aiding your preparation.

Note the conditions

Once you have determined the distance of the shot you intend to play, note the slope of the ground and any hazards that may come into play, such as an out-of-bounds line, intervening rough, ditches, trees, bunkers, hillocks and/or water.

Now judge the weather conditions. Is it windy, and if so, from what direction is the wind blowing and how hard? Is it raining, or has it been wet in recent days? Is the ground damp or dry? Soft or hard?

With all that information, you should be able to gauge how the ball will fly and whether or not it will run very far on landing.

Deciding types of shot

Now it's time to bring everything together and decide on the type of shot to play – a draw or fade, high or low – and to imagine the flight of the ball.

DECIDING ON THE SHOT TO PLAY

Making the right decision as to the type of shot you are going to attempt is an essential part of playing a good golf shot. Spend some time evaluating your shot, especially when you are in trouble. And only play a shot that you have already practised.

BENDING THE BALL

Later chapters explain how to hit the 'draw' and the 'fade', essential shots for the advanced golfer. A draw moves from right-to-left with a low, penetrating flight and will run considerably after landing, leading to extra distance. A fade moves left-to-right, flies higher and lands softly, resulting in less distance.

Deciding what type of shot to play is largely down to experience and knowing your own capabilities. However, if you are a beginner, you might seek advice from a caddie or playing partner – unless you are in a club competition, when seeking advice from a partner is against the rules of formal play.

Now put everything together.

Perhaps there's a big tree on the left of the fairway about 100 yards (91m) from your present position, while past that the ground slopes away from you in the same direction towards the green, which in turn is about 160 yards (146m) from where you are. In such a situation, the ideal shot would be a right-to-left draw, enabling you to bend the ball around the tree and then take advantage of the run you will get from landing on the slope.

Being creative

In the same circumstances, if your natural shot is from left to right, or a fade, you might have to be more creative. Perhaps the solution is to take a more lofted club than you originally intended in an attempt to fly the tree and cut off the dogleg.

Now it's a matter of not only distance, but of getting the right height on the ball, and perhaps sacrificing a direct attack on the green, hoping you can then chip up and take one putt for par.

Visualize the shot in your mind, getting a real 'feel' for the shape of the ball's flight, how it will be affected by the wind conditions, how it will land and how far it will roll after landing. Then select the right club for you and take a few practice swings. Don't just brush the grass with your clubhead. Line up the way you will for the actual shot, and practise with an eye towards your intended swing path. That's where your set-up comes into play.

SHOT SELECTION

ABOVE Some shots are inevitably more difficult than others. Be confident in the shot you choose.

THE LIE OF THE BALL

ABOVE If you have a caddie, discuss the shot and agree that the one you have chosen is well within your capabilities.

LEFT The lie of the ball can make a shot easier or considerably more difficult. Evaluate the lie before deciding on the shot you are going to play.

THE PRE-SHOT ROUTINE — THE SECOND PHASE

The second and final phase of the pre-shot routine comes after you have sized up your situation on the golf course and decided what shape of shot you would like to play.

Some golfers think they are ready simply to take aim and fire at this point. But no pre-shot routine is complete without two more small, but vital, additional elements:

1 Finding an intermediate target.

2 Relieving muscular tension.

Stand behind your ball and visualize the ball-to-target line, choosing some feature a short distance ahead to use as an aid to aiming your shot at the target. This might be a twig, leaf, divot or clump of grass. But the key is to find something close to the ball. It's always easier to line up with something nearby, rather than something far away.

Moving around to the side to address the ball, hold the club in your right hand and place the sole of the clubhead behind the ball, aiming the face down the short ball-to-target line you have selected.

Now take your stance, assuming the correct posture, flexing your knees, and lining up your feet, hips and shoulders — again, parallel to the short ball-to-target line you've selected — and just as in the railway track analogy used earlier in the chapter when we were looking at the Set-up.

Finally, checking that the clubface is still aimed correctly, add your grip.

Relieving tension

Here comes the toughest part of all. Prior to starting the swing, pressure can become part of every golfer's game, from beginner to hardened pro. If you're facing an important shot, or lack confidence in what you're about to do, muscular tension can creep in and destroy your swing action.

Getting rid of that swing-strangling tension can make the difference between a clean, crisp hit that flies to the target and sets you up to score well and a violent hook into the trees.

So rid yourself of any rigidity by lifting the club and giving it a waggle or two. Then wiggle your toes inside your shoes, or move your feet up and down in a little

WAGGLING

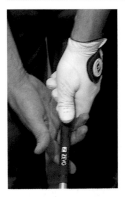 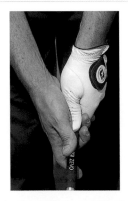   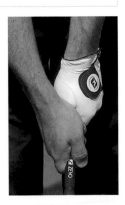

Tension in the set-up usually begins in your hands. Waggling the club while setting up to the ball is the best way to relieve this tension and prepare to swing.

RELIEVING TENSION

LEFT The nightmare scenario – don't let tension destroy your golf shot.

BELOW Moving your feet up and down at set-up is also a great way to keep the body loose.

Waggling the club is done just with your wrists. The shoulders and the rest of your body do not move, otherwise you may alter your set-up position.

PRO TIP

The waggle is a vital ingredient of any pre-shot routine in order to relieve tension and groove the feeling of your swing. But some golfers take that a step further. Let's say you've decided to play a draw shot. In this case you could use your waggle as another form of miniature rehearsal. Bring the clubhead back just on the inside as you waggle – the same way you will when you begin the in-to-out swingpath of the draw – then take it slightly out before assuming your final address position.

tap dance. Flex your fingers on the grip, letting any tightness drain away, which will also help release any tension in the wrists and forearms. Finally, try to capture a feeling of lightness and relaxation throughout your arms, shoulders, legs and torso.

Now glance one last time at the target – focusing for a split second – before resuming your normal head position at address.

A mini-rehearsal

You've now completed the pre-shot routine. If you learn to do this consistently, you should automatically begin to play better golf. After all, the pre-shot routine is a mini-rehearsal for the swing itself, and thus a vital way of making that swing count. Such a routine is as important as the swing itself, and is a prerequisite to achieving overall consistency in your game.

At the heart of the game is one central action – the golf swing. Developing a repeating and athletic swing that holds up under pressure is a key to success on the golf course.

THE BACKSWING

Making the first move is a key in any sporting activity – and especially in the golf swing. Like a sprinter about to explode from the blocks, you have to be both poised and ready to go, yet relaxed enough to unleash your full power smoothly. A smooth, fluid beginning to the backswing is the key to a powerful, genuinely athletic swing.

In the previous chapter, we explained how to assume a solid grip, a balanced and dynamic set-up – or stance – and a pre-shot routine that can help ease tension and serve as a mini-rehearsal for the real thing. Now it really is time for the real thing.

The first move in the golf swing is termed the backswing. Get this part right, and you have built the foundation for a powerful, athletic swing. But get it wrong, and nothing good can follow. The backswing is the key to the swing itself – which in turn is the central action of golf.

Start without a golf ball

So how should you approach the first move? First, you must fully understand what your body will be doing in the backswing, then programme it accordingly through hours of practice. Initially, much of this practice will not involve hitting any golf balls. Simply picking up a club and heading for the driving range is a recipe for disaster.

THE FIRST MOVE

The first move in the golf swing is the most important part of it. A low, slow takeaway will help ensure that your arms, hands and body move in one coordinated movement.

In order to teach your arms and body to move together, try placing a credit card between your left arm and ribs.

The right arm should not be held as tightly to the body, so a clubhead cover should be placed under your right armpit.

Ensure that when you initiate your takeaway, you rotate your body immediately.

So, don't go near a golf ball...at least for now. If you are a beginner and want to learn how to swing the club properly, this is the best advice you can receive. And if you are an experienced player — but have had limited success — it's even better advice.

The role of your body

Understanding the role of your whole body in the swing is crucial. Most golfers concentrate on the hands, wrists and arms, whether consciously or not. But unless you fully comprehend the role of the large muscles of the upper torso, hips and legs in the golf swing, and how they work together with the arms, hands and shoulders, you'll never learn or master a proper swing.

By understanding this physical combination, you'll begin executing the first move in a way that will put you in the correct position at the top of the backswing. In turn, that will allow you to start the downswing — or throughswing — in the most efficient and powerful way possible.

The end result? You will propel the ball towards its intended target with both accuracy and length, setting up the possibility of a good score. If you have not mastered the basic technique, the first move will cause you problems and lead to any number of golfing disasters.

DON'T FREEZE UP

Once you have gone through your pre-shot routine and assumed your stance, don't stop — as so many golfers do — by grounding the club behind the ball and going into a trance that leads to muscle tension. Pull the trigger as quickly — yet smoothly — as possible.

DEVELOPING A REPEATABLE SWING

You may know the feeling: you are standing on the first tee, and your playing partners are waiting for you. The next group is standing nearby, watching and waiting, eager for you to get off so they can start their round. In addition, there is out of bounds on the left -- maybe it's the club car park.

At such times, it's very easy to get tense and even freeze over the ball, especially if you lack confidence in how to make that first move. If this happens, you are in big trouble. Add a faulty technique to the mix, and you'll really wish you had stayed at home.

The repeatable swing

Here's how to avoid that nightmare scenario and hit a great shot — over and over and over again. By making the correct first move, you will prepare yourself for what's called the 'repeatable' (as in reliable) swing.

Once you have mastered this basic movement, you are well on your way to that goal, because the repeatable swing is just that — repeatable. It will not break down when you are tired, nervous, exposed or otherwise under pressure. You'll play better overall — and if your temperament is right, you'll even start winning competitions.

Now that dream round is closer to reality, but only if you can make the first move properly.

The basic swing

The swing is, of course, one continuous, athletic movement. But in order to understand best how it works — and how you can make it work for you — we'll examine the swing in two parts, breaking down each element of the backswing and throughswing until you thoroughly understand each.

After that, we'll put it all together and study the finished product, the complete swing — a swing that you can take to the course. A swing that you can start working on that will eventually produce consistently lower scores.

Golfing secrets

Learning the proper swing is the only way to unlock the basic secrets of golf – which is equally true for the beginner and the professional. Yes, even pros are constantly learning about the swing and retooling their basic movement.

Tiger Woods and Phil Mickelson are two pros to have benefited from a change of approach in recent years, while a few pros – notably Nick Faldo – have even scrapped a successful swing and completely revamped their basic action. Along with golf guru David Leadbetter, Faldo completely remodelled his swing, using many of the basic ideas and techniques described in this chapter.

The result was a better swing under pressure and increased success on the golf course.

You can do the same.

STARTING FROM SCRATCH

In the early 1980s, Nick Faldo was the top-ranked golfer in Europe. But Faldo knew his swing hid a multitude of faults that wouldn't stand up under the pressure of the world's 'major' tournaments. So he approached British coach David Leadbetter, who told him the refit would mean almost completely scrapping his swing, a process that could take at least two years – during which his game, and his earnings, would suffer.

Faldo was determined to become one of the world's best golfers, so he plunged into the task with relish, often practising such long hours that his hands bled. Faldo failed to win any tournaments in 1985-86 and critics began to doubt his ability to regain his form. But in 1987, as he finally became more comfortable with his retooled swing, the discipline began to pay off and it became clear that he had emerged as a technically better player. After capturing the Spanish Open, Faldo snatched his first major, coming from three behind at Muirfield to defeat American Paul Azinger for the Open Championship.

In the years since, Faldo has won a host of tournaments in both Europe and the USA, plus two more Open Championships and three US Masters, to bring his tally to six majors. He also holds the record for the number of points and matches won in the Ryder Cup.

THE REPEATABLE SWING

A repeatable golf swing is the result of a good set-up combined with a smooth, unhurried rotation of the body with the arms forming a wide arc throughout the back- and throughswings. Practised regularly, this will become a consistent movement.

THE CONNECTED SWING

Tee up the ball, take your grip, assume your stance, and go through a pre-shot routine. Now you are ready for that first move into the backswing.

Before making that first movement, it's important to conjure up a feeling of lightness throughout your body, but especially in your hands, arms, shoulders and upper torso. At the same time, your legs need to be poised and stable – but never rigid – evenly distributing your weight in order to support a dynamic movement away from the ball.

Next, think about making that first move with a nice feeling of rhythm and tempo, easing into the backswing in a way that builds towards a consistent, overall swing, and ultimately the release of maximum power into the ball.

Finally, you want to tie all of the above sensations together in a low, slow and smooth movement – what I like to call the 'connected' swing.

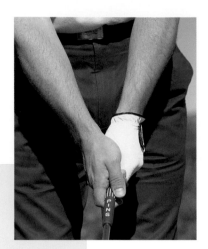

A light grip is essential to building good movement.

LOW AND SLOW

The best advice when promoting the idea of the connected swing, while also establishing a nice sense of rhythm and tempo, is to start the takeaway – the first move – with the clubhead being taken back from the ball very low and slow. Start the club an inch or two above the turf and move as slowly as comfortable, concentrating on a smooth movement. This promotes the idea of the arms, hands, shoulders and upper torso moving back together and the club staying on the proper line.

A movement that is slow and smooth keeps all your body parts together, avoiding the tendency to snatch the club away with the hands. Taking the club back low to the ground also helps widen your swing arc, allowing the bigger muscles to impart more power to the ball later in the throughswing.

ASSUMING THE STANCE AND FEELING CONNECTED

Here you can see the arms, hands and upper torso moving together, both on the back and forward swings.

REAR ANGLE CONNECTION

A light connection of the upper arms and body aid a consistent movement.

Feeling connected

Your hands, arms, shoulders and upper torso should move together, turning back and coiling behind the ball – partly in opposition to the lesser turn of the hips (more on that later) – while they are anchored by the stable foundation provided by the legs.

This feeling of connection is the secret to building a consistent, athletic golf swing that will repeat time after time – and, most importantly, under pressure.

By tying in the hands and arms with the larger muscles of the upper body, a motion that is fluid, coordinated and dynamic can be produced. In turn, that will generate the maximum amount of clubhead speed in the downswing, as you hit through the ball to a high and stable finish.

If you lose that feeling of connection at the beginning of the swing the entire action will fall apart.

Staying connected

The vast majority of golfers I see tend to move their arms and hands independently of the rest of their body, or upper torso. That is why they struggle for

consistency in their swing. And even those who have been taught the connected swing – or who have read about it – sometimes struggle to get it right when practising it.

Often this is because they go to the opposite extreme, taking the idea of connection too literally. They interpret it as meaning that you must lock everything together, rather than just moving the various parts of the body together.

In each case, a golfer will never be able to reach his or her full potential.

Only halfway

Connection will not work unless you are relaxed and can maintain a feeling of lightness throughout your upper body. And without good rhythm and tempo, you will have the lightness, but you won't have dynamic movement.

Remember, the backswing merely sets up the full swing. Do it right, and you're halfway there. But only halfway. As the great Bobby Jones once said, you don't hit the ball on the backswing.

TRIANGLE-CENTRE DRILL

This drill helps to ingrain the idea of connection throughout the swing. If you do it correctly, it will give you a strong impression of how the hands, arms, shoulders and upper torso ought to move away together from the ball – and how they work together as unit.

For this exercise, you need to choke down on a club (in other words, grasp it further down the shaft than normal) and place the butt end against your body, somewhere between the navel and sternum – whatever feels most comfortable. Then practise moving the club away from an imaginary ball until the clubhead is about waist-high.

The most important part of this drill to note is that the last thing to reach a finished position at waist-high is the clubhead.

Did that surprise you?

If so, you are like so many other golfers. You have been swinging with the hands and arms, rather than the body. But in this exercise, it is the connection that moves the clubhead to its destination. Probably, in the past, you have been moving the clubhead in a way

that leaves your body catching up rather than driving the action of the backswing. It is now time to reverse that damaging tendency.

Tail wags the dog

Jimmy Ballard, the famous golf guru, describes this initial move as a way of maintaining a feeling of the 'triangle and centre'. He, and others such as the legendary Ben Hogan, have traditionally taught that, at address, the relationship between the shoulders, arms and hands should form a triangle that remains unbroken throughout the entire swing.

With the butt of a club against your torso, you will sense how the body's 'centre' – or the middle of the upper torso – stays in harmony with that triangle. In other words, the large muscles of the upper torso

BELOW This simple exercise will help you understand just how the arms, hands and upper torso work together in the rotation back and through.

TRIANGLE CENTRE DRILL

move in conjunction with the arms, hands and shoulders in the connected swing, pulling the clubhead back and through the ball.

Put yet another way, this time by David Leadbetter, the 'tail wags the dog'.

The one-piece takeaway

You might have heard the first move of the backswing being described differently – as the 'one-piece takeaway'.

This expression is potentially confusing to many golfers, and not just to beginners. Because of the image it conjures up, it is inevitable that golfers interpret it by almost pushing the club back with the hands, arms and shoulder joints.

Do that, and the only way to raise the club fully is by cocking the wrists too soon, and in a way that lifts the arms across the chest. Thus, you are making the first move without the centre of your upper torso being involved, and you are breaking the connection that you need to strive to maintain.

The first move in the golf swing must be made with the triangle of hands, arms and shoulders in unison with the centre of the upper body. This is fundamental to the golf swing.

RIGHT If the arms work independently of the upper torso and rotation does not occur, the result will be a choppy swing resulting in a sliced, pulled or skied golf shot.

Supple and connected

When the club is waist-high in the backswing, the left arm should be comfortably extended and supple, so that if someone came along and pulled the club down to where you would normally grip it, you would remain connected and have a full extension of the clubhead.

At the same time, the right arm is starting to move away from the body and fold naturally.

If you were to continue the backswing here, the right arm would establish a triangle with the left up to the top of the swing, further mirroring the position at address when viewed from behind.

BELOW The triangle-centre drill also helps you to appreciate just where the club should be halfway back and halfway through in your swing. Perform this exercise regularly.

TRIANGLE CENTRE DRILL - REAR ANGLE

PRACTISING THE CONNECTED SWING

Now let's put the triangle-centre drill to good use in the swing. Swing the club back to the waist-high position and stop. It may feel odd having the butt of a club against your chest, while assuming the position of such a short swing.

Beyond that, any discomfort or restriction you might sense is almost certainly down to the fact that you have never swung a golf club in the correct manner before – in other words, you might never have taken the club away from the ball in the first move of the backswing with your hands, arms, shoulders and upper torso working together in the connected swing.

Now try doing the drill again, but this time do so without consciously keeping the butt of the club against your chest.

What's the betting that very shortly after moving away from the ball, the butt of the club has parted company with your body?

If this happens, it's a sure indication that you have gone back to your usual swing – that you are making the first move with the hands, arms and shoulders, while your upper torso lags behind or even doesn't move at all.

If your movement is a series of independent moving parts, instead of a connected swing, your swing will lack consistency.

Practise correctly

Now go back to practising the drill correctly, doing it over and over again to ingrain the idea of the connected swing. Use a long mirror if you have one, or better still, videotape yourself and note the progress you make.

It's important to concentrate on the idea of 'connectedness'. Think about how the body – in this case the upper torso – moves the hands, arms and shoulders, rather than the other way around.

Note also how your weight shifts back to your right foot and your left knee turns back towards the right – which we'll discuss further later.

PRACTISING THE CONNECTED SWING

This is a great exercise to develop good rotation on the correct plane. Take your posture first and then practise turning while at the same time staying bent over. It is important not to lift up or dip down – just rotate.

PERFECT TAKEAWAY

In a perfect takeaway there should be no hand action as you initiate your swing.

CONNECTED SWING CLOSE-UPS

The natural hinging of the wrists will occur if you maintain a light pressure in your grip. As you rotate, your right arm will fold naturally as shown above.

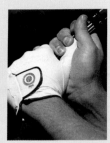

The momentum of the swing will cause your wrists to cock naturally.

Cocking the wrists

Unless you are an absolute beginner, you are probably wondering why I haven't mentioned the role of the wrists in the first move of the backswing.

I'm sure you will have heard golfers talk endlessly about how and when to cock their wrists in the backswing. Or maybe they talk about how to manipulate their hands in the throughswing, especially at impact if they are trying to hit something other than their normal shot – say a draw. You may have even been given some 'friendly' advice such as this during a round, delivered with the guarantee that it will improve your game immediately.

Passive hands

This might surprise you, but you should forget anything and everything you have ever heard about cocking the wrists and turning the hands!

The hands remain passive during a connected swing. They respond to everything else being done correctly. In a properly connected backswing, the right arm will begin to fold naturally as you reach waist-high, and the momentum you are starting to build with the club will cause a natural hinging of the wrists.

If the club is gripped in the correct manner, and your swing is connected – with the triangle taken back with the centre – the wrists are set in the proper position automatically.

So take it from me. Never make a conscious effort to cock or otherwise turn your wrists during the golf swing. Never!

POWER AND CONTROL IN THE CONNECTED SWING

Shifting your weight correctly is a key to building a powerful swing. In order to understand this, you should resume the position you had with the club waist-high in the triangle-centre drill with its butt pressed against your chest.

The connection you've established should have caused the left knee to break in well behind the spot where you would have set up to the ball, and your weight should have shifted until it is predominantly on the inside of the right foot, or at least over the right foot from about the centre to the heel.

If neither is the case, go back and do this again until you feel the proper weight shift and can establish that position – while also keeping the right knee as flexed as it was at address.

Now swing through to a waist-high finish – or, put another way, swivel forwards to face your intended target. You should feel your weight shift completely to your left foot, with a feeling that your right foot could lift off the ground with little or no effort – if it has not done so already.

By now you should also be starting to gain the sense that the throughswing *mirrors* the backswing.

Clubhead position

If you perform the triangle-centre drill correctly – including a proper weight shift between feet – you will see that the clubhead remains in the right position, not just when you take the club back but also when you swing it through.

Assuming that you had the clubhead square at address, and did not manipulate your wrists, you should find that at waist level in the backswing the toe of the club points upwards to the sky, with the leading edge perpendicular to the ground. The clubhead should be in the same position at waist level in the throughswing.

In other words, the clubhead should be square.

WEIGHT TRANSFER

Open toe

If you find that at waist level in the backswing the toe of the club is open – or pointing behind you and facing up – this will indicate that you did not maintain your connection in the swing and that you probably tried to dictate what your wrists were doing.

By the same token, if you find that the face of the clubhead is pointing towards the ground, or closed, in the throughswing, this will also mean that you have broken your connection between the triangle and centre. Breaking the connection makes any chance of

returning the clubhead square to the ball at impact considerably more difficult. You will also lack the proper coil behind the ball, because you have shortened the arc of your swing.

That almost inevitably leads to various mishaps as you instinctively struggle to bring the clubhead back to square with your hands. It will also lead to a lack of power in the swing.

Body leverage

The point of all this is to introduce you to the idea of body leverage in the connected swing. By using your body to swing the golf club, you create power and consistency. This will give you a much stronger movement through the ball and you will not have to exert as much energy.

Watch the average golfer at the range. Within minutes, he's grunting and sweating. Does your favourite pro do that? When he or she swings, the effort looks minimal, and yet the result is a powerful, controlled shot, epitomizing what we mean by the phrase 'playing within yourself'.

Loss of control

Most golfers, whether consciously or not, think they can create power through their arms and wrists. They try to whack the daylights out of the ball, short-circuiting any input of the larger muscles of the body. This has several negative consequences, the most common being a disconnection of the swing, and thus a loss of control over the clubhead.

If your swing is dominated by the hands and arms, the clubface will open and close too quickly and you will be unable to visualize where it is at any point of the swing. The tendency to try to compensate for the clubhead being in the wrong position is difficult to resist for any golfer, and inconsistency will dominate your ball-striking.

When you use a connected swing, you move the clubhead in tune with your body, and it will open and close much more slowly and be in the proper place throughout the swing. In effect, there is less to do, and less to worry about, in the connected swing – and the result will be greater consistency.

LEFT The rotation of your body combined with the transfer of your weight from right foot to left foot is the engine of your golf swing. If you want a powerful, elegant and efficient golf swing, learn and practise good body rotation and weight transfer. Observe players like Tiger Woods – he is the best golfer in the world because he understands body leverage and connection.

HEAD POSITION IN THE CONNECTED SWING

The first move away from the ball will break down if you become fixated on the ball by trying to keep your head still or down. Your goal should be simply to allow your head to rotate freely with your body rotation.

Don't allow the ball to become the absolute target, otherwise you'll end up in all sorts of trouble. Think about your swing, and where you want the ball to go, rather than the ball itself – partly by not staring fixedly at the ball, and partly by letting your head rotate slightly on the backswing.

Transfixed by the ball

But we sometimes forget this. Standing over that little white orb, we are sometimes reluctant – or plain terrified in the case of many beginners – to turn the body, and thus the head as well, behind it.

We become afraid of losing visual contact with the ball. We become convinced that the very act of keeping both eyes staring down will somehow ensure that the clubhead returns to the correct position, enabling a clean strike of the ball.

But the outcome will be quite the opposite, because failing to move the head will prevent the correct body movement and destroy any hope of a connected swing. So forget everything you've ever heard about keeping your head still.

Head rotation

Not moving the head is one of the great myths in golf. In fact, the head must rotate slightly back, or to the right, along with the upper torso in the connected swing. So, that feeling of lightness we strive for before the first movement in the takeaway should extend to our neck muscles as well.

The neck muscles should be relaxed. They should be receptive to movement.

Keeping the head in a fixed position, or square to the ball, will cause the swing to break down as the left arm folds up and collapses, reducing any chance of imparting real power to the ball. That's because you will be unable to turn fully behind the ball, so you will reduce the width of your swing arc.

In order for your body to rotate back and through, allow your head to move with your body. At the top of the backswing you should only be able to see the ball through your left eye, the head should then rotate through so that you finish looking at the target.

CORRECT HEAD MOVEMENT

Address.

Top of backswing.

Just after impact.

Finish position.

Head myths

I wonder where the myth of the 'steady' head came from, or what other commentators sometimes refer to as keeping the 'head down'.

The correct practice has always been not to keep the head still, but to maintain some visual contact with the ball – acting on the basis of that other old sporting adage, 'keep your eye on the ball'.

This maxim really does apply, although what we actually want to happen is to see the ball with only – and I emphasize 'only' – the corner of the left eye. You can test this by taking a practice swing and closing your left eye at the top of your backswing. If you can still see the ball, you've got a major swing fault as there is certainly no 'connection' in your swing.

Again, you have not turned fully and your swing arc is narrow.

Swing trigger

Study the tournament pros on television and it will become apparent that all the great players move their head in the backswing, some more than others.

Jack Nicklaus often tells the story of how his first teacher used to hold his hair in order to stop him from turning his head. But in fact, Jack always did turn his head, though in his case, he moved it before he started the backswing, pre-setting it so the corner of his left eye is over the ball before he starts his movement.

For Nicklaus, that move is a swing 'trigger'.

Lateral movement

These days, several great players not only rotate their heads to keep their swings connected but also work on a slight lateral movement of the head.

Tiger Woods is a good example. By the time he has set his powerful swing at the top, his nose is just over the inside of his back foot, with his head very much behind the golf ball.

So before you even start the swing, tell yourself that your head will move. Allow for the natural rotation of the head as the upper torso moves to the right and back, allowing the body to coil behind the ball. Then forget everything you have ever been told about trying to keep your head still.

HEAD-DOWN DISASTER

Forcing your head to remain still or down on a golf shot is the worst thing you can do.

NEW TOOLS OF THE TRADE

Having a friend videotape your swing is really the only way to check your head position during the entire movement. Computer software used while teaching pupils even allows for multiple images of your swing, including those shot from various angles, to be studied on the screen simultaneously. This marvellous tool also offers the option of comparing what you are doing with images of other golfers – it's helpful being able to compare images of golf pros practising on the range with those of pupils, focusing on players who have a similar build and physique.

Lateral movement makes good striking impossible.

THE FOUNDATION OF YOUR SWING

Another point that often gets overlooked before we even start our swing is the role of the lower body. Your weight should be distributed from the balls of your feet to your heels, and it should remain this way in order to provide a solid, balanced foundation for the entire swing.

But many golfers get utterly fixated on their hands and the ball sitting below them on the tee or grass. And since they are holding the golf club in their hands – and the clubhead is poised near the ball – that's where most of their attention is directed.

They are concentrating only on what they can see right in front of them.

Supple legs

I try to have a definite sense of my legs supporting me from below – supple, and yet firmly in contact with the ground, and, of course, connected to the rest of the body.

If you do not have this feeling of support, your central nervous system is liable to interpret that as a sign of instability down below. And if that message is sent to the brain, the result will be a certain rigidity, as your body rejects any idea of cutting loose in a strong, athletic movement.

It's a bit like standing on one leg.

If you do that, your body will try to find a way to brace itself to overcome the feeling of instability, and this will certainly prevent you from doing anything as powerful and dynamic as swinging a golf club, for fear of the obvious result – you will lose your balance and topple over!

Your legs play a crucial role in anchoring your swing. Like a building, a golf swing needs a stable foundation.

LOWER BODY

LEGS AND SUPPORT

ABOVE LEFT TO RIGHT In order to maintain the plane of your golf swing and to brace the upper body rotation, your legs must retain the same flexed position as at address throughout the swing.

BELOW If the lower body does not provide good support, loss of balance will be inevitable.

THE BACKSWING – PUTTING IT ALL TOGETHER

The correct backswing should feel more or less natural. The movement should be programmed into your mind and body. Let's go through the process together.

HOGAN'S LAW

Ben Hogan said that he did not care if a golfer raised his left foot in the backswing or not. And some of the great players had a pronounced lift in their front foot. But, if at all possible, keep your left foot planted. It is one of the keys to a powerful, athletic swing.

Once you know what your target is, you want to feel strong, relaxed and prepared to make all the right moves. Then you initiate your first motion in the backswing by trying to keep things very smooth, with a continuous, easy flow of the hands, arms, shoulders and upper torso away from the ball.

Simple pictures

Picture the 'centre-triangle' image again, with your shoulders forming the base, your arms the sides, and your hands the apex of the triangle. You want to keep this triangle intact as you start the backswing, relative to the centre of your chest.

After you have practised the essential parts of the first move repeatedly, finally it's time to simplify things. Just think in terms of maintaining the same basic position you had at address throughout the initial part of the first move. In other words, you can now drop the idea of the 'centre-triangle' and picture instead a mirror image of a good address position being held throughout the backswing.

Dynamic resistance

Meanwhile, the lower body will be braced and supporting your movement, with the weight starting to move onto your right foot and the hips gradually being pulled around by the turn of the upper torso.

Note that the hips are turned around by the upper torso. They follow, rather than move simultaneously, or lead the action. If this movement is done correctly, a slight tension will begin to build between the hips and upper body – and, in this case, the tension is good. Such tension is dynamic, the resistance that actually balances the whole backswing, while later

providing – by opposition – a powerful coil as the body moves fully behind the ball and begins to build up the power you will later unleash through the golf ball.

Coiled spring

What does one mean by 'coil'? Think of your upper body as a spring, turning against the resistance of your hips and legs. At the top of the backswing, that spring should be fully wound up, ready to be unleashed – or sprung – in a powerful throughswing that fires through the ball to a high and balanced finish.

As you move through your backswing, keep in mind that your hips actually end their rotation at roughly a half turn of the shoulders and upper torso.

Remember also that it is the upper torso which pulls the hips around. They do not rotate at the same time or pace as the upper body. In fact, they are the last major part of the body to move in the initial phase of the backswing.

Weight transfer

Weight transfer is also a vital part of the backswing. You want to transfer most of your weight to the right foot as you rotate or turn back from the ball. By the time you finish the first move, about 90 per cent of your weight should be over the back foot, distributed from the centre to the heel.

At the same time, your right knee should remain braced and flexed, just as it was in the set-up. This provides the support needed to hold your position at the top, although that will only take split seconds.

Meanwhile, your left foot has stayed on the ground – a little lift of the foot here is acceptable, as long as you do not become unbalanced.

To become a good golfer you need to study the previous pages so that your backswing can be produced automatically. Then, when faced with that pressure shot, you will instinctively believe in your movement.

THE ATHLETIC SWING

The basic golf swing has changed dramatically in recent years, becoming more and more athletic. Players now have the ability to impart more stretch and torque – or coil – to their swings, and that, in turn, gives them considerably more power.

The great golfers of the future are likely to be professional athletes able to hit the ball up to 400 yards (365m) with a driver. One of the secrets of achieving this is keeping the left foot planted on the ground in the backswing – while completing your rotation. Doing so adds resistance, and therefore power, to your overall movement.

Maximizing power

What does one mean by an athletic swing? Think of it as a strong, yet pliable and stretchy motion. Your body is used like a piece of strong elastic, which you stretch, then let go, the way you would fire off a giant rubber band or spring.

Making the body work in this way maximizes your power. Some golf instructors like to describe this as 'coil' or 'torque', and that is the essence of the modern swing. Today's players are trying to make a more

The athletic swing is the swing of the future. But remember that power is only an asset if it is combined with accuracy.

powerful movement than ever before, while striving for consistency.

This is the magic formula for success. If you can have great power with consistency, you have an unbeatable combination.

Driving averages

Today's great players, such as Tiger Woods, can routinely hit the ball over 300 yards (274m) with accuracy. Only 30 years ago, the average driving distance among professional golfers was about 250 yards (229m). Yet now it's about 280 yards (256m). Advances in equipment have helped this surge, but so too have more advanced training regimens, including dietary and lifestyle considerations.

Today's players are stronger and fitter. They are, in fact, true athletes, which they must be in order to compete in the modern game. To perform the swing

THE ATHLETIC SWING

of a Tiger Woods, you have to be both very physically strong and supple. And while not everyone can work towards an accurate replica of such a swing, the average golfer can produce a movement that is at least something like it, allowing them to maximize their potential.

Swing variations

Variations on the basic golf swing work for both pros and amateurs, but be cautious about emulating another golfer's technique or traits.

For example, the Spanish golfer Sergio Garcia tries to think in terms of stretching his left arm to create more width through his left side. But if the average golfer were to try to stretch his left arm a bit more – in an attempt to get a lot more width – the likely result is that he would become too tense and disconnect his swing.

For the mere mortals of this world, it is better to concentrate on the connected swing, with hands, arms and body moving together, rather than just stretching one part of your anatomy. If you are going to try to copy another golfer in one particular respect, at least focus on someone who shares your height and build.

Shaking hands

Here's one idea you can use. The American professional Tom Kite has a wonderful way of helping golfers visualize the movement in the backswing. He says you should imagine you are turning around to shake someone's hand.

Notice how much emphasis there is on the opening of the upper torso when you do this – you are almost turning around to face backwards. And if you can picture turning back to shake someone's hand who is in front of you, that is a nice description of how we return to the impact position, and then move through to the finish.

That's the kind of opening in the golf swing that most golfers should strive towards.

Being strong and fit can only be an asset to a golfer of any age. Why not enrol in your local gym and develop a fitness, toning and stretching routine based around your golf swing? You'll be amazed at the results.

BACKSWING PROBLEMS

Many golfers interpret the idea of turning away from the ball on the backswing as requiring an almost complete body turn. In other words, they move their hips along with their shoulders and upper torso — rather than allowing the upper torso to pull the hips around. When they do this, they fail to create any dynamic tension between the upper body and the hips.

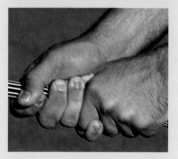

Tight hands will kill any chance of making a good swing or feeling the clubhead.

That is all right in the beginning. In fact, if most golfers did that, they would be better off than not turning their bodies sufficiently. If you are going to overdo it, that's the way to go.

But the real problem for the majority of golfers is that they do not open the body enough, if at all. In fact, the vast majority always underdo it.

Opening fears

The fear of turning away from the golf ball is a persistent problem for most golfers. They simply do not rotate the body at all, or they do so to a minimal extent. In other words, they simply lift the club with their arms and hands. As a consequence there is a very limited opening of the torso, and a very small amount of weight transfer, and that is extremely damaging to the swing.

Most amateur golfers also overswing by using their arms and hands too much in the beginning of the backswing, and then they add a bit of rotation. But because they have used their hands and arms independently to begin with, before turning slightly, they end up with their arms and hands over the top of their heads, and the left arm inevitably breaks or folds.

If they had opened the torso correctly — and really been committed to that action at the beginning of the movement — their problems would vanish. The crucial point is to make sure that the arms and hands are passive in the first move — in fact, almost totally inactive. I cannot stress that enough.

RIGHT When you are standing over the golf ball, it's vital that you are preparing your body to move. Too many golfers get stuck at this stage and end up like mannequins over the ball, unable to move freely.

HEAD DOWN, STRAIGHT LEFT ARM

How often does one see this? Head down, straight left arm – it's a disaster from which few recover. How can you possibly enjoy the game playing like this?

Straight arming

Another of the great myths about the golf swing is that you must always keep your left arm straight. Gary Player was a great proponent of this, but then he was one of the most coordinated and physically fit golfers who ever played the game.

But Player was also small, and in trying to find additional power, he devised a backswing technique that gave him more width.

Loosen up

The idea that you should not break the left arm does not mean keeping it rigid or stiff. In fact, it certainly should not be rigid or stiff.

Many great golfers – Seve Ballesteros comes to mind – have played the game at the highest level with a swing that had a certain amount of give in the left arm. Remember, it is the big muscles of the upper torso that are really driving the golf swing and providing the power to hit the ball. So the arms really have a far lesser role to play.

There is nothing wrong with having some break in the left arm, as long as it is not caused by independent movement of the arms and hands, a movement made without the rotation of the body.

The USPGA tour pro Calvin Peete is a great example to illustrate this. He actually has a withered left arm. But when he turns, he keeps everything together, and as a result he was one of the most consistent players on the PGA tour during the 1980s.

UNLOCK YOUR ARM

Slavishly trying to keep the left arm straight in your backswing can stifle any free, athletic movement in your overall swing and may even cause injury. When a golfer tries to keep his or her arm straight, they often twist the elbow inwards at address – rather than more naturally bowing the elbow out slightly. With the elbow twisted in, the golfer will struggle to return the clubface to square at impact and probably hit a hook. Even worse, some golfers smother the ball, slamming the clubhead into the ground, which not only results in a bad shot, but can also send shock waves up the arm – eventually damaging either the wrist or elbow.

SPINE ANGLE AND SWING PLANE

When you take your position at address, you have effectively preset your spine in a certain alignment – what pros call the 'spineangle'. As you rotate your body in the swing, it is essential that the angle you have created at address is maintained throughout the swing – so there is absolutely no lifting or lowering of the spine.

If the spine angle varies, it will have a very detrimental effect on your ability to bring the club back through the ball towards the target. So it's essential to maintain the spinal angle that you created at address.

Fixed axis

Picture an imaginary line drawn down your back, from the top of your head to your hips. As you begin your backswing, you are rotating your spine around that angle, or line, turning back and then forwards, opening and closing your body in relation to this fixed axis.

It is similar to a door hanging on an angle from a pair of hinges – opening and closing. That is how the body turns along the spine angle, both in the backswing, and as we unwind through the ball.

At the same time, your shoulder turn should remain perpendicular to your spine, and your shoulders turn on a level plane, with the hips on roughly the same line. This is what we call the 'swing plane'. The swing plane both follows from, and is connected to, the spine angle.

ABOVE LEFT Developing a consistent swing plane is very much part of becoming a consistent striker of the ball.

LEFT Your posture will determine your eventual swing plane, therefore make sure you're in a good position before taking the club back.

In the slot

What do we mean by 'swing plane'? Ben Hogan was one of the most consistent strikers of the ball in the history of the game. But even he struggled to 'slot' his club into the proper position at the top of the backswing until he understood the idea of 'plane'. Once he grasped that concept and practised swinging the club along this imaginary line, he gained enough confidence to rely on his swing in the pressure of competition and eventually to become a winner of golf's most coveted trophies.

Imagine a pane of glass extending from the ball to your shoulders, with your head poking through a hole at the top. The angle of this plane will vary depending on your height and the distance that you stand from the ball, producing what we often refer to as either a steep or shallow plane.

Staying on plane

One thing is constant. There is no such thing as a swing that is too steep or too shallow if the golfer consistently swings his shoulders along the line of the plane. Like the spinal angle, any variation above or below the plane will put the swing out of position, which in turn will lead to a bad shot. But staying on the same plane throughout the swing will groove an excellent movement.

Try to think about both your spinal angle and swing plane when practising your backswing. Getting both right is one of the essential ingredients of making that first move correctly.

Once you are confident you can make that first move, you'll be like a sprinter poised and ready to explode out of the blocks when the gun goes.

BELOW A simple way to understand the swing plane is to swing the club at a target, in this case a caddie's hand, positioned at different levels, starting at head height and working down to the ball.

REFLECTIONS ON SWING PLANE

You can check to see if your swing plane is correct simply by looking in a mirror. Pick a spot on the floor where your ball would normally be in your address position, then swing a 5- or 6-iron back, holding it at the top. If an imaginary line drawn from the butt end of your grip to the ball falls across your left shoulder, your swing plane is too upright. This means you probably return the clubface to the ball in an open position, take deep divots, and often sky the ball. If the imaginary line cuts across your navel, your swing plane is too flat and you probably return the clubface in a closed position, resulting in many shots hit too low and hot. The correct – or neutral – swing plane places the imaginary line directly across the right shoulder. From there, you will return the clubface square at impact and strike the ball more consistently, leading to greater success on the golf course.

THE THROUGHSWING

Now it is crunch time. The transition from the top of the backswing to the start of the throughswing is the most crucial split second in golf – and the ultimate moment of truth.

PRACTISING THE BASEBALL SWING

A simple baseball type action is good practice when you are first developing the correct turning motion though the ball.

With the body coiled and ready to unleash the clubhead at high speed, the release of power into the ball on the throughswing can either be an exhilarating experience or an embarrassing hack.

Either the golfer will take advantage of having achieved an excellent position at the top of the backswing – with the body fully rotated and powerfully coiled behind the ball – or the golfer will now destroy all his or her previous good work.

Executed properly, the throughswing will unleash the clubhead at high speed – the pros hit the ball at over 100mph (161km/h) – smacking into surlyn or balata to send the ball flying high and true towards the intended target.

Taking short cuts

On the other hand, the golfer may make a terrible hack of the job, not only embarrassing himself but perhaps doing permanent damage to his score. How many times have you seen a fellow golfer make a nice backswing, only to snatch the club back at the ball or fail to hit through it?

The failure of most amateur golfers is caused by rushing – they are trying to short cut the downswing. They're nervous. They want to get to the ball as soon as they can. So almost instinctively, they fall back on old habits, bringing the club down with their hands and arms, rather than using their body.

Looking easy

The transition phase from the backswing to hitting through the ball must be a dynamic, athletic move, fully utilizing the body in a coordinated fashion that is seemingly unhurried, and outwardly graceful. Whether scoring a goal, hitting a boundary or sinking the winning basket, the very best sportsmen and women make it look easy – even if it is anything but – and that is the same in golf.

Uncoiling the swing

So, learning how to perform the throughswing is a case of disciplining the body and brain through practice. The golfer must know what is about to happen, and how he or she should proceed.

Simply put, the throughswing is a reverse image of the backswing, as the legs, hips, upper torso, shoulders, arms and hands gradually uncoil piece by piece. At the same time, there is a slight lateral weight shift to the left, as the majority of the weight moves from the back foot to the front.

In other words, the swing uncoils in exactly the same order as it was previously coiled up, so that the last thing to go back is the first thing to come forward.

Image and feel

Think about that for a moment. Images and a physical feeling for what we do in golf are vitally important. As with many of the things we have looked at, I would suggest that you first practise this movement in front of a mirror with a club, but no ball. That's the best way to help you prepare for what you'll do later on the practice range — and ultimately on the course.

I like to focus on the impression of the backswing uncoiling like a tightly wound spring into the full swing. I firmly believe that if you can think of this move in that way, it will help to unravel any mystery attached to the throughswing — and help it unfold in a logical sequence.

Don't stay down with the ball too long, otherwise you'll get trapped behind the ball.

THE THROUGHSWING - BAD FOLLOWTHROUGH

PAUSE AT THE TOP

One of the most common faults of the average golfer is the tendency to hit from the top – or initiate the throughswing with the shoulders, rather than allowing them to uncoil gradually after the lower body starts to move back to the left. The legendary Tommy Armour, a Scot who emigrated to America in the 1920s and won 24 golf tournaments in two decades – including both the US and British Open – developed the most famous cure for hitting from the top – a split-second pause at the top of the backswing. In his 1953 book *How to Play Your Best Golf All the Time*, he wrote that adding this pause was the 'greatest single aid' to eliminating what he saw as the 'worst fault in the golf swing'.

Next time you are at the golf range, try Armour's technique and see if it doesn't help improve the timing of your throughswing.

THE FIRST MOVE FORWARDS

It can be difficult to keep the first move in the throughswing under control – just as it was difficult to make that first move in the backswing.

Most golfers, when they realize that they have arrived at, or near, the top of their backswing, suddenly want to get the clubhead to the ball as quickly as possible. Try to resist that.

So relax, there's no need to rush, the ball isn't going away. The throughswing has to be smooth, so that the body can uncoil fluidly and pull the clubhead through, rather than the other way around.

First move forwards

Remember that as you coiled up your body in the backswing, your upper torso and shoulders rotated back, your weight shifted from your left side to your right side, and your legs provided balance and support for the entire movement.

At the same time, this coiling motion pulled in the left knee, inclining it towards the back leg, while the hips were gradually pulled around to half the rotation of the shoulder turn.

It follows that the first part of the body that should come forward to start the throughswing is the left side. I believe that a slight lateral movement of the left hip towards the target is the ideal trigger, or first move, for your throughswing.

In the past, golfers as eminent as Ben Hogan and Bobby Jones also thought that the forward turning of the hips was the trigger that initiated the throughswing.

Other golf pros and swing gurus maintain it is actually a separation of the left knee from the right, the shift of weight onto the left foot.

It is difficult to focus precisely on individual actions, since they happen so quickly and everyone has their own way of sensing this motion. On top of this, any swing that is truly athletic will be partly instinctive, and will vary slightly from golfer to golfer. The way a golfer perceives the sequence of what happens will inevitably vary.

A slight lateral movement with the left hip towards the target initiates the forward move. As your hips rotate to face the target, your upper body and clubhead will be pulled forwards developing tremendous centrifugal force.

THE FORWARD MOVE

THE LOWER BODY

Suffice it to say that the hips and left knee move more or less simultaneously in the first split second of the throughswing and weight is transferred to the front foot.

Uncoiling the body

The essential point remains that the body must uncoil gradually, roughly from the ground up, in reverse order to the backswing coil — with the movement of the clubhead always coming last.

If you watch a slow-motion replay of a good swing, you will see that there is a pronounced separation of the left knee from the right in the initial part of the throughswing. Roughly at the same time, the hips and upper torso are beginning to uncoil as well, pulling through the shoulders and arms as the weight transfers smoothly from the right foot to the left.

The overall effect is that these actions allow the body to rotate around the left heel into the final part of the swing.

Forward power and drive

The way I like to think of this first move, and the way I teach it to my golfing pupils, is by telling them that they are trying to develop a strong sense of forward power and drive, thus imparting that energy to the ball. This starts with a slight lateral movement of the left hip, which goes forward towards the target, then this translates into a rotational movement that pulls the body around, letting it eventually open up fully to face the chosen target.

It should be emphasized that this action must be done in the most non-violent way possible. The initiation of the throughswing should be an easy and fluid move, because if you turn the left hip — or anything else for that matter — too aggressively, the club will be thrown outside the correct line and you'll hack at the ball with an out-to-in swingpath, probably slicing it as a result.

Remember, the uncoiling of the body into the throughswing should be a natural movement that you do not force, hurry or try to push. A good way of thinking about this is to focus on the idea of simply *letting it happen.*

ABOVE In order to develop the correct motion through impact, practise turning your left hip to the left whilst at the same time swinging the right hand towards the target.

ABOVE The forward drive of your lower body is an essential part of developing a powerful golf swing.

THE THROUGHSWING FROM IMPACT TO FINISH

An essential ingredient of both the backswing and throughswing movement is the efficient transfer of weight. In order to initiate the throughswing, you have to get the weight back over to the left side in order to unleash the swing and provide power to the clubhead.

Using a slight lateral slide as the hips begin to turn and the knees separate, you rotate over the left heel, holding the club lightly and simply letting it swing through. In effect, you should allow the club to pull you. If that happens, you're really in business. But if you start pushing the club in any way, you will have serious problems.

Hard work

What is meant by 'pushing' the club? Instead of allowing the club to swing freely with light hands and wrists, many golfers try to muscle the clubhead into the ball, which inevitably means that they are holding the club too tightly and forcing all the action. In other words, instead of the club doing what it was designed to do, you do all the work.

Of course, your reward for all that hard work is a golfing disaster.

Club pull

As the body continues to rotate to the left, the club is literally pulling the golfer through to a complete follow-through.

Try to hold the club as lightly as possible and allow the left hip to ease its way around in the throughswing. Don't try to be aggressive. Let your weight naturally move onto the left heel, and set the clubhead free.

If you have done all of this correctly, and allowed the club to swing freely, centrifugal force will come into play and pull the arms to full extension. Yes, the club will actually pull you, and you might even be able to feel the right shoulder being brought through under your chin to its finish point.

Impact!

What happens when the clubhead finally smacks into the ball? The answer may surprise you – very little that you need worry about. If you've done everything correctly up to this point, the clubhead will merely zip through the ball and send it 300 yards or more – if you're Tiger Woods, that is.

Any conscious effort to manipulate the hands or wrists will only lead to trouble. At the impact position, you can do precious little to control the clubhead, because everything is happening too fast. Rely instead on a sound grip, your preparation and the proper execution of your swing to allow the clubhead to do the work at this stage.

Practice images

I would suggest focusing on several images that you might conjure up when practising. These will help you to visualize your position at impact, and how you groove your movement through the ball.

First, think of swinging through the ball as something like throwing underhand to a target, a bit like skimming a stone across a pond. The right arm is at first coiled backwards and raised, then swings forward with the wrist providing that extra momentum as the stone or ball is released. At the same time, the elbow passes close to the right hip and finishes with full extension or beyond.

Practise doing this with a tennis ball, a stone or whatever is available to give you the right feeling, then grab a club and swing it to waist-high. Think about the right hand turning over the left on the throughswing – once past impact.

THROUGHSWING
Here you can see the throughswing in action. The hips are turning left and the club is released towards the target.

Although the throughswing is very much about freedom and letting the club 'go', the relationship of the arms and body remains constant. Swinging a heavy object such as a medicine ball, or in this case a cool-box, helps develop the feeling of the arms and body working together throughout the movement.

Two-handed pass

Of course, you want to swing as freely as possible with both hands through impact. One way to ingrain this idea is to practise with, ideally, a medicine ball, or a football or basketball. Imagine you are making a two-handed pass with the ball, from right to left, the object being to get the ball to a target. Doing this resembles the motion of the golf swing.

Hold the ball in front of you and take your address position. Then begin a simulated backswing. You will automatically shift your weight from the left foot to the right, which builds up your power, then reverse the action as you fling the ball towards the target.

Natural power

This exercise will give you the idea of how you can naturally generate power in the swing through simple body leverage, with the hands and arms serving as conduits of that energy. In the end, your body rotation will carry you all the way around to the left, in exactly the same way as the club does in a good swing.

But remember that, at impact, your technique is what you must ultimately rely upon. If you make a

good backswing, and unleash your throughswing in the proper sequence, you will generate energy and power at the point of contact, with the centrifugal force mentioned earlier controlling much of what happens through the ball.

The finished position

How do we get to the finish of the throughswing? Simply put, the rotation of your torso and shoulders continues until your hips are fully turned and your chest faces the target, the body having fully rotated around your left heel.

That's the part that should be common to everyone. And yet every golfer has their own version of the finish, and they can vary dramatically. Some are unusual, and some are absolute works of art. Think of Arnold Palmer. Then think of Ernie Els.

The point here is that while no two golfers finish their swing in quite the same way, they all tell us something about what went on before. They provide an insight into a golfer's strengths and weaknesses, giving us clues as to how we might enhance the good points, while fixing the faults, in our own swings.

Maintain the finish

It's a good idea to maintain your finished position for a few seconds. You want to do this because:

• If you anticipate finishing up with a balanced, controlled follow-through, that will have a positive effect right through your golf swing.

• Your swing faults will become apparent so it will be easier to monitor your swing. If you fall forwards at the finish, for instance, you will discover that you did not shift your weight properly and you were therefore unbalanced.

This is about programming the body and brain to know what they are trying to achieve together. Such visualization techniques work on the subconscious. Thinking about balance and control will impart the proper idea while you are actually moving the club.

Count to three

At the end of the golf swing, you should hold the finish and count, 1-2-3.

But rather than thinking of this as a finale, remember that the real action in golf is only just beginning. As you count, the imaginary ball has started to rise into the air and fly towards your target.

Exhilarating swings

If you have done everything described in this chapter properly, the experience of hitting a golf ball *will* ultimately be exhilarating, rather than embarrassing. In short, you will have released the power in your swing, and found the key to unlocking your potential for the game of golf.

Before we conclude our examination of the swing and you try to take these techniques to the course, please read the following pages where I pull together everything about the backswing and throughswing, then round it off with a few more mental images. I also offer some final tips and thoughts on the central action of your game – your golf swing.

As the swing continues through, these pictures featuring both cool-box and golf club show how the arms, hands and torso maintain the relationship that began at address.

THE COMPLETE SWING

Now the time has come to draw all the bits and pieces together to form your own dynamic and athletic swing, free from conscious thought.

For your swing to repeat you must learn to 'feel' your swing rather than 'think' your swing. Practising blindfold or with your eyes closed will quickly help you to understand just how a good swing should feel and help you to trust your movement.

It's so easy you could do it with your eyes closed. How many times have you heard that one? But, in truth, we often make life more complicated than it is.

At the heart of the game is one central action – the swing. Hand a golf club to a three-year-old, and that child will probably come up with a pretty good approximation of a proper golf swing.

Hand the same club to someone who has been playing the game for years and they will begin thinking – and, if they ever do finally take a swing, in all likelihood they will make a complete hash of it.

Now hand the club to a pro, and watch him or her make one smooth, seemingly effortless pass at the ball to produce a drive that seems to fly forever or a high fade that lands the ball softly on the green 85 yards (93m) away, a few feet from the pin.

Instinct and practice

What's the difference between the three golfers?

Two of them can swing a club with their eyes closed, because they perform the action in what appears to be the most natural and instinctive way. Of course, in the case of the child, it *is* instinctive, while in the case of the pro, it's a mixture of instinct and about a million hours of practice.

Throughout this chapter, we have been looking at the backswing and the throughswing and dividing each of these into separate parts. Now is the time to link the parts together and show you how to make the complete golf swing 'simple'. So simple, in fact, that it becomes natural – something you could even do from time to time with your eyes closed.

Which is how I want you to start.

BLINDFOLDED SWING

Remove the ball

The first step to learning the complete swing is to remove the ball from the equation. Remember, you are trying to programme your body to move instinctively back from the ball, then through the ball to a high, balanced finish. But, invariably, the golf ball draws attention away from the real action of the swing, almost putting the average golfer into an hypnotic trance.

If that happens, any natural opening of the torso in the backswing will be inhibited and the swing motion might begin to disintegrate, destroying any hope of a properly executed, complete golf swing.

I try to counteract that tendency in my pupils by asking them to take slow-motion swings without the ball, swinging over and over again to build confidence in their movement.

At the same time, I tell them to discipline their bodies to move properly, to ingrain an understanding of what they are trying to achieve.

Doing it with your eyes closed

Now comes the interesting bit. After you have swung the club slowly for a time, make some more swings with your eyes closed. In fact, make hundreds with your eyes closed. And while you do this, concentrate on how the various movements in the swing feel, how they come together, and how they combine with the action of your body.

See? You *can* do it with your eyes closed.

Swinging in this way will also emphatically prove something else: that, although earlier we broke the swing down into its various parts, in reality it should be one continuous, flowing motion.

Putting it all together is about developing one continuous, flowing motion that is smooth, unhurried and consistent. Now you're ready to shoot those low scores.

REPLACE THE BALL

Nick Faldo spent the first two months of his golfing life developing his golf swing without a golf ball. When he began hitting balls, he had already created a swing that consistently propelled the clubhead towards the target.

Repetition is the mother of skill. And remember quality is better than quantity so practise good swings again and again.

What is the natural extension of the concept of removing the ball? My own golf instructor, Ian Connelly, used to repeat one basic rule over and over again to me. Only after you have learned how to swing the club properly are you ready to bring the ball back into play – and, finally, into its proper role.

In other words, you have now ingrained the idea into your mind and body that the swing is the central action of golf, and that it should be your principal focus – not the act of hitting at the ball. So after you've developed a dynamic, athletic swing, just put the ball in the way. I repeat: just put the ball in the way.

A good golf swing is one in which the ball is simply in the path of the clubhead. The ball is not your target.

You merely swing through it, with no conscious effort to hit it. If you can master that concept, you have taken one of the biggest steps possible towards finding your own complete swing.

Instinctive golf

Like the little child who grabs the club and swings away with youthful abandon, you have to learn, or re-learn, how to be instinctive about your swing. An excellent swing links physical know-how and mental application, then tosses away the conscious mindset of the technician.

What do I mean by that? By now, your swing should be mechanically sound, but also programmed

A MUCH IMPROVED SWING

in your subconscious, with the whole process written into your muscle memory and throughout your body. Of course, unless you continue to practise, any consistency that you have achieved up to this point will start to deteriorate.

Repetition and skill

Go back to what I said before. You must swing the club in slow motion, over and over and over again, without the golf ball. Far too many golfers fall into the trap of thinking they have learned something, and then immediately head out to the range, eager to whack a couple of dozen golf balls.

Avoid that trap like the plague. If you try to short-circuit the process, it will be disastrous for the development of your swing. You have to develop a pattern, and that takes hundreds of hours. Repetition is the mother of skill.

That is how to become consistent and to learn how to *not* think about the ball and the parts of the swing. In other words, how to make the swing instinctive again.

EXERCISE

REMOVE THE BALL

Former Ryder Cup captain Bernard Gallacher recommends golfers to turn the brand name on the ball down to avoid fixating on the ball, especially when teeing up. This way, the golfer sees only a clean, white area. Any number of problems can result when a player stares at the ball. He or she might limit their lateral movement in both the backswing and throughswing, or the head may come down, creating a rocking or tilting action. Gallacher says he tries to play with a simple awareness of the ball below him, almost seeing the ball only in his subconscious.

If you can't practise regularly, perform simple loosening exercises that remind your body of the correct movement.

CENTRIFUGAL FORCE

The concept of centrifugal force is useful when it comes to understanding the complete swing. If you put a weight at the end of a piece of string and whirl it around, you will create motion in the weight that is much faster than your wrist can move as it twirls the object. We've all done that as children.

You might also think of this idea in terms of figure skating, where the man spins his partner quickly around him, as if he were an axis point. Even though he does not move particularly fast, she is able to move much faster than him once they have built up enough force and rotation.

Try to think of the golf swing in this way, with the clubhead the weight at the end of your string, or the skating partner at the end of your arm.

Pulling arms

Once I enable a golfer to create a good shape to his or her movement in the swing, I tell them to keep their hands as light as possible and try to sense the feeling of spinning that weight around them, the force coming from the centre of their body, which in this case serves as the axis. If they can harness this strength and force properly, the clubhead will pull their arms to full extension.

Any tension will destroy the effect. The arms will narrow and the swing arc will lose its width. This is like moving your wrist when spinning the weight on a string. The weight will drop out of its orbit and slow down or even stop.

The same happens in the golf swing when you don't allow the club to swing freely, or you move out of plane. The hands and arms take over, the power and momentum you have created is reduced, and your shot will lose distance and accuracy.

Radiating power

What is the secret to maintaining centrifugal force in the golf swing? Remember that you must coil and then uncoil your body in a smooth, efficient manner to produce a good swing. Do that, and you will radiate power out from the centre of your body – or torso – while at impact you will be able to whip the club through the ball.

The hands and arms must be passive in this situation. They conduct force and energy, but do not generate it.

Think of how a discus thrower uses his athletic skill to propel the discus a great distance. He winds his body up in a circular motion from the ground up, concentrating and shifting his weight. His hands and arms merely serve first to hold the discus, then to transmit the energy he is slowly building. Finally, he uncoils his body fully and seems to explode into the final movement, the discus hurtling from his grasp.

Rotate ahead

How can you relate this to your golf swing? Keep in mind that the discus thrower is always turning ahead of his discus, and that everything involved in his physical technique happens before the discus leaves his hand.

That's what you want to do in the golf swing as well. You want to turn or rotate your body ahead of the clubhead, in effect keeping the clubhead behind your motion, so that the lag builds up tremendous force and drive into the ball.

The ball then goes a great distance.

OPPOSITE If you allow your club to swing freely, your arms will be pulled to full extension by the centrifugal force developed by the swing.

BELOW As you can see in the top left picture in the sequence below, by this stage the club has taken the initiative and is pulling you to the finish position shown in the final photograph.

ANCHORING THE SWING

What is the axis of the golf swing? On the previous pages I described how a golfer can generate force and energy in the swing from the centre of the body, and how he or she can rotate around that as an axis point.

But the axis point of an individual's golf swing is not like the fixed position of the wrist when a weight is spun around on the end of a string. Neither is it the same as the upright partner in the graceful movement of a figure-skating pair.

In a sense, there is more than one axis point in the anchoring of the golf swing.

At address, our weight is evenly distributed between the left side and right side. But when we move into the backswing, we shift our weight to the back foot, then transfer it forward to the front foot in the throughswing.

This shift, plus the coiling of the upper body against the more static hips and legs in the backswing, produces power that is imparted to the ball.

So the axis, or anchor, of the swing is really two contact points – our feet.

Pivots and turns

Golf guru David Leadbetter calls the basic motion of turning back and through in the golf swing a 'pivot'. Others simply call it a 'turn' or 'rotation'.

Whatever term you prefer for the basic movement of the golf swing, the one constant is the role of your feet. If they don't provide a solid foundation for the swing, you will become unbalanced and the entire action will unravel.

You should always keep the weight distributed between the middle of the feet back to the heels. When you move your body in the swing, think about rotating around each of your feet.

Putting that in the simplest way possible, your axis points are your right and left heels. On the backswing, you first shift your weight to the right foot, then you should start thinking about swinging around the left heel on the throughswing.

Coiling behind the ball

Offer any golfer three wishes, and what would he or she ask for? The answer would probably be distance, distance, distance.

But if you asked most golfers to demonstrate how *they* think increasing their distance can be accomplished, the vast majority would probably produce a swing that is mostly hands and arms. Their solution would be a vain attempt to muscle the ball down the fairway.

The secret to executing a powerful, dynamic swing is a coordinated physical effort that starts with the move away from the ball. At the top of the backswing, the body must be fully coiled like a spring, ready to snap back and unleash the clubhead through impact with the ball.

In other words, most golf swings are only as good as the backswing the golfer uses to set up his motion. The key to understanding how to do this well is knowing how far to move behind the ball.

When you make your backswing, feel yourself rotate round the right leg. Here my colleague ensures that my right knee remains flexed throughout my backswing. Do the same with your left knee on the follow-through.

ANCHORING THE SWING

Reverse pivot

Imagine a short wall behind your right leg. Now swing back until you have fully coiled your upper torso and hips behind the ball. If you have done this properly, your leg should be snug against the wall. However, if you have gone too far back, you have swayed past the wall and have lost the effect of using your right leg as a brace for your weight, and a help in enhancing the athletic energy of your coil.

On the other hand, if your right leg never moved into the wall, you have probably produced a reverse pivot, the 'cardinal sin' of golf. In a reverse pivot, the weight actually tilts forward onto the front leg, so that when you start your downswing, your weight will then move back onto your right foot. The result will be any number of variations on a bad shot, and a dramatic loss of distance.

PRO TIP

As an aid to body rotation, think about how your right knee, although flexed, should swivel slightly during the backswing. If it points to 12 o'clock at address, it should have turned to 1 o'clock as the body moves back from the ball. The knee rotates slightly to allow the body to turn. If the back foot is slightly opened up (i.e. turned outwards), that helps rotation as well, aiding the opening of the body.

The same is true for the front foot. Both can be slightly open, despite what you may have heard in the past about the back foot needing to be perpendicular to the target line, while the front foot is open.

Having both feet angled out is a more natural set-up for most players.

ABOVE AND RIGHT Good support in my lower body ensures that my coil will be secure so that I can realize my full potential when swinging the club through the ball.

Remember – turning the feet out slightly will aid the opening of your body both back and through the swing.

REVERSING A REVERSE PIVOT

How can you avoid the reverse pivot and make a proper backswing? Take your stance with the ball roughly opposite your left heel and start your backswing. Now imagine a vertical line running from the centre of the ball up to the sky. If, at the top of the backswing, you are totally behind that line, your coil is correct.

PRO TIP

Many golf instructors stress turning with some lateral movement to get weight onto the back foot. But how much is enough? As a practical matter, a full movement behind the ball almost never happens anyway. Everyone who has ever taken a golf lesson knows about turning behind the ball, but few golfers necessarily get all their weight shifted to the right side, then back to the left on the throughswing.

Simply put, try to get as much weight transfer as you can. Don't worry about swaying off the ball, since you are probably doing the opposite. If anything, the body has a tendency to get stuck over the ball. So fight your fears and you'll achieve a better overall swing.

The failing of most golfers, however, is that they become anxious as they move away from the ball and never fully turn behind it – in other words they fail to 'complete' their backswing.

A good backswing

Remember that in order to achieve a good backswing you need first to turn the triangle of the hands, arms and shoulders back from the ball in conjunction with the centre of the upper torso.

At the same time, there is a slight lateral movement to the rear as the weight shifts and the hips and left knee are pulled back by the chain reaction set up by your upper body – until everything settles into the brace of the right leg.

Uncoiling the body with power

The throughswing then starts in reverse sequence to the backswing, from the ground up, as the hips turn back and the weight moves to the left heel, pulling the upper torso, shoulders, arms and finally the hands – which should remain passive throughout, following the orders being issued by the body.

This, in turn, lets the clubhead lag behind slightly, building up tremendous power and centrifugal force until it whips through the ball and continues into a high finish.

Think of this as an uncoiling of the body. After winding up the dynamic tension in the body, you are now unwinding it – in much the same way as a boxer throws a punch.

Of course, he does not start his move with his weight forward. Rather, he subtly winds himself up by shifting his weight back, then moving towards his target with the stored energy of that weight shift.

THROWING A PUNCH

Convincing a player to move behind the ball is the most difficult part of my job. Imagine throwing a punch or skimming a stone – the move backwards is the 'power move'.

LEFT Reverse pivoting simply means moving your body weight the wrong way round. In a good move your weight should move to your right foot in the backswing and the left foot on your follow-through. So if your weight is on your left foot at the top of the backswing – start to worry.

BELOW A good finish position generally indicates a good backswing. A swing should mirror itself on the backswing and throughswing.

Multiple sins

The failure to coil properly behind the ball creates a multitude of problems. If a golfer does not complete the backswing, he or she will have a tendency to begin the throughswing from the top, rather than the bottom up, and so cut across the swing plane.

In doing this, the swing becomes disconnected, and the relationship between the centre of the body and the triangle of the hands, arms and shoulders is destroyed. Now the hips are swivelling with no real role to play and the club is thrown or almost cast like a fishing rod.

This generally guarantees that the clubhead will return to the ball in an open position (i.e. pointing to the right of the target line) and the golfer will hit a weak slice. But, given this scenario, the hands might also turn over, and then a dead pull is produced.

In better players, the swing path of the club will not be quite as badly affected, but the disconnection will certainly prevent an adequate release through the ball. Distance and accuracy are always sacrificed because of this faulty move.

SWING KEYS

There are common traits in every good golf swing, and they should be studied and practised over and over again in order to groove a repeatable swing.

A brief pause at the top of the backswing can help to maintain a good rhythm and tempo in your swing and aid consistency.

BELOW Making the first move is never easy. Try kick-starting your swing by moving your right knee towards the target together with a slight rotation of your hips in the same direction.

Here is a checklist of some of the most important factors that you should bear in mind as you prepare to swing your golf club:

• In the set-up, the feet should be spread to shoulder-width (measure this from the inside of the heels) and the hands, arms and shoulders should form a triangle, with the left arm and club extended in virtually a straight line.

• Knees and hips should be level. The right shoulder will be slightly lower than the left as the right hand is lower in the grip.

• The spine should form roughly a straight line from the top of the head to the hips, with the backside jutting out slightly as a balance point.

• A little flex should be present in the knees, giving the feeling of standing tall to the ball.

• The body, especially the hands and arms, should be free from tension. A controlled waggle or two just before the ball is struck, plus a wiggling of the toes or slight lifting of the feet, will help to ease tension.

Kick start

I recommend David Leadbetter's way of initiating the first move of the swing. He suggests a 'kick-start' from the right knee towards the target, in conjunction with a slight rotation of the hips in the same direction. Practise this move until it becomes ingrained.

A brief pause

Some golfers have an almost perceptible pause at the top of the backswing. In fact, the body is really moving in two different directions at this point. As the backswing reaches its fullest turn, the lower body starts to move forward. Taking a brief pause at the top will help steady your swing and make it more consistent. You will also aid your rhythm and tempo, and probably keep your swing in the proper plane.

Standing tall

With the proper emphasis on the body moving first in the throughswing, rather than the hands or arms, the impact position will resemble that of the address. The golfer will appear to be standing tall again, with the left arm fully extended. Any dip or break of the left arm at this juncture will ruin the flight of the ball.

Mirror image

A good swing should mirror itself in the way the body turns back and through the ball. Try to develop a feel for how the swing reflects itself by practising slowly in front of a mirror or video camera. At the same time, try to think about how to simplify all the various parts of the swing into two basic moves – the body turning away from the target, then turning towards the target.

Try especially to think about how the body dictates the swing, with no thought given to the role of the hands, arms or the ball.

KICK START

HOW TO PRACTISE

Most golfers cannot wait to start letting fly with a bucket of golf balls after they have read one magazine article on swing technique, taken a few lessons, or tried a new grip. That's a recipe for failure.

BELOW Learn from your divot pattern – with clubs lined up on the ground it's easy to see if your swingpath at impact is good or bad.

Even if you do hit a few good shots, it would be a mistake to believe you have mastered a new swing, or some aspect of a new swing. More than likely, you'll probably hit a lot of indifferent shots after the initial excitement wears off. And again, it would be a mistake to think that fact means anything, either good or bad.

You have to practise each new aspect of the swing for a considerable period of time before you can incorporate it into a practice routine, and certainly long before you can take it to the course.

Driving range tips

Do go to the driving range, although, once there, try not to hit too many golf balls. Take lots of practice swings instead. And use an easy club like a 6-iron, rather than the driver, for an extended time. After you have built up some confidence, and an understanding of what you are trying to accomplish, then you can pull out other clubs, trying to groove the same swing aspect with each.

Always aim at something when hitting balls on the driving range and vary the targets – because when you play, you are confronted with different situations.

Develop and practise a pre-shot routine at the range. Top pros have a consistent routine that helps them visualize the shot, take aim and relax before hitting the ball. Developing consistency in one area will work into other parts of your game.

Time for success

Pick a target, decide on what club to use and how to shape the shot, then visualize the ball moving along your target line and landing where you want it to go.

Move behind the ball to find an aiming point, using something a few inches ahead on the mat or grass.

Take your stance and give the club a waggle to loosen up before starting your backswing.

Finally, step back and see how many other people at the range are doing the same thing. Not many, I'll bet, which is their mistake, not yours. Now you're ready to take a shot.

Go ahead, and succeed.

HOW TO PRACTISE

Good = straight shot.

In-to-out = slice or push.

Out-to-in = hook or push.

Practise with all your clubs, hitting a variety of shots. This keeps practice interesting and helps you become more creative on the golf course.

The only person you never see in golf is yourself. That's why you need a good teacher.

4 CHIPPING AND PITCHING

Devote 50 per cent of your practice time to these shots
and your scores will improve dramatically.

CHIPPING AND PITCHING

Have you ever played a round with a golf pro? If you have, you know what separates their game from yours. It's not their distance off the tee or their silkier putting stroke – it's their short game.

Put another way, it's how they correct errant shots. How they get the ball up and down for par after making that occasional, but inevitable, mistake. Meanwhile, when you go into a bunker, miss the green by a few feet, or face an awkward 40-yard (37m) pitch, you know you're probably heading for bogey (one over par) – at best.

The same holds true for the pros out on the various tours around the world. Think of today's leading stars, and who do you come up with? Golfers who combine awesome power off the tee with an exquisite short game. Pros like Tiger Woods, Ernie Els, David Duval, Colin Montgomerie, Laura Davies, Annika Sorenstam and Karrie Webb are all considered 'long', but also have 'touch' around the greens.

BELOW Pros often carry different types of wedges from the rest of their irons (3–9 irons). These wedges are often made of softer metal to help control the golf ball from short range.

BOTTOM There are even different shafts made specially for wedges that are stiff flex and that maximize the feel of the clubhead.

The real secret

Now you know the real secret of golf. In this chapter, and the following two on bunker play and putting, you will learn how to play better from close in, a skill which can dramatically lower your scores.

But there's a catch. You'll have to practise these shots more than you probably do now, because here is where feel and, to some extent, imagination come into play. That does not come easily, though any extra time you spend perfecting these shots will more than pay off in the long run.

As Gary Player – one of the great short-game artists of all time – often says: 'The more I practise, the more I get lucky.'

The standard pitch shot

The pitch shot is a crucial shot for the average golfer for all the reasons stated above, and for one more reason in particular.

Most high- to medium-range handicap players will generally miss at least 50-60 per cent of greens 'in regulation' – by which we mean the number of shots a low handicapper is expected to need to reach the green. In other words, the high handicapper might have problems hitting the green in two on long par 4s and certainly most par 5s.

In each situation, the golfer is often faced with a third shot which a pro never has to play, which accounts for the 18 or so extra strokes that the average club player is given in the form of a handicap before his or her first tee shot on the first hole.

But here is where you can cut that margin down and start threatening the club championship, or at least move up in your local rankings. With a solid pitching stroke, you can start turning bogeys into pars, and pars into birdies.

Floating pitch

How many times have you found yourself with 200 yards (185m) or more to an elevated green for your second shot on those long par 4s? And how many times have you faced an 85-100 yard (78–91m) shot on a par 5 for your third?

In the first case, most golfers would be advised to forget trying to hit the green in two and put that problematic fairway wood back in the bag, opting instead to hit a comfortable 7- or 8-iron to a spot around 100 yards (91m) or less into the green. Alternatively, with the modern development of utility woods, other players may opt to try a 7- or 9-wood and try to land within 40-60 yards (37–55m).

In both cases, you are now ready to float a high pitch shot onto the short grass. With practice, you should be able to land that pitch close enough to the pin to have a chance at making the putt.

Ball position will vary depending on the height that you require on the pitch shot.

BELOW LEFT Practice will help you determine the length of swing required for various distances.

BELOW RIGHT The chip and run shot can be used if no hazards lie between you and your target.

PREPARATION FOR THE PITCH SHOT

The pitch shot is really just a miniature version of a full swing. The ball is hit high because of the loft of the clubhead – usually travelling between 35 and 100 yards (32 to 91m) – and goes further in the air than it does along the ground.

Set up with your ball in the centre of your stance and your hips and feet pointing slightly left of the target (open stance). Your shoulders should remain parallel to the ball-to-target line. Your hands should be ahead of the golf ball and you can choke down on the club (by how much depends on the length of shot).

The most commonly used clubs to play the pitch shot are a sand wedge, a pitching wedge and a 9-iron. The choice of club will very much depend on the distance you need to carry to the green.

The pitching wedge – usually about 48 degrees in loft – is the highest lofted iron in a standard set of clubs, with additional wedges available in increasing degrees of loft. In recent years, many golfers have also added a lob wedge to their bag, ideal for shorter pitches off a good lie.

Short but sweet

Now for the tricky part, and the reason why you must spend more time practising this shot than most others. The pitch is hit with an abbreviated version of the full swing, but the ball must still be hit firmly. Put another way, although you are not swinging the club as far back as you would for a normal shot, you must still accelerate at the bottom of the swing, just as you would for a normal hit.

Without an authoritative swing, you will pull your punch, and the result will be a disastrous hit, a shot skulled over the green or one that trips along the grass seeking out a hazard. Now, instead of that par or birdie you envisioned, you're looking at bogey, double bogey, or even worse.

As a result, many golfers fear the pitch shot as much as any other in the game.

PITCH SHOT TECHNIQUE

The standard set-up

There's no reason for that fear if you understand how to execute the pitch shot.

The key to making a good pitch is first to set up well to the ball. Here, the stance is a miniaturized version of what we use for a longer iron or wood, with some important differences.

The first difference is that the stance for the pitch shot is more 'open' than for other shots, which means you need to pull your lead foot back from parallel to the target line by a few inches. At the same time, the back foot, hips, chest and shoulders should remain square, or parallel to the ball-to-target line.

The second difference is that the stance is narrower, with the outside of the feet at about shoulder-width for the average pitch – for a 5-iron, an imaginary line would run from the outside of your shoulders down to the inside of your heels, this distance widening slightly for the woods.

The third difference is that you should position your hands in front of the ball, choking down slightly on the club, leaving about two inches (5cm) of the grip protruding from the top of your linked hands.

Weight and posture

Now you are ready to distribute your weight according to the type of shot you are about to play.

If you are hitting a pitch from 80 yards (73m) or more to the green, you should favour the left side with about 55 per cent of your weight and your right side with about 45 per cent. If the shot is closer to the green, perhaps only 35-70 yards (32–64m) out, the weight should be even more towards the left foot, at a ratio of about 60:40. With less weight transfer, you are able to exercise greater control over the shot and get the ball closer to the target.

As for posture, that is determined by the club you have selected for the shot.

With a sand wedge, for instance, you will be more bent over than if you were using a 9-iron, because the wedge has a shorter shaft. Therefore, you will need to sit back more – or stick out your rear end – to keep your balance throughout the swing, simply because your spine angle is more inclined.

LEFT AND BELOW When you play the pitch, your weight should favour the left with less weight transfer. This will help you control the shot and get the ball close to your target.

Ball position

For a standard pitch shot, position the ball in the middle of your stance or even slightly further back, depending on how high you want the ball to fly. This is explained further under Advanced Techniques, along with variations on the standard pitch, such as the lob over a hazard, the low-flying pitch under the wind and pitching from the rough. But for the average pitch, setting the ball halfway between the feet is the ideal.

MASTERING THE PITCH SHOT

Now that I have shown you how to assume the proper set-up for the pitch shot, let's take a look at the basic swing action, which is similar to the normal golf swing but has a few marked differences.

Placing your hands down the grip is one way of controlling distance on your pitch.

Good tempo is crucial in mastering the pitch. The first move should be low and slow.

The technique used for a pitch shot is very similar to the normal golf swing but there is less weight transfer, the backswing and throughswings are more compact and the emphasis is on accuracy.

Your left hand is one of the keys to the throughswing. This hand must stay ahead of the clubface, then remain ahead of the right hand for as long as possible. At impact, keep your left wrist firm — but not rigid — and focus on striking the back of the ball. It's important not to scoop or chop at the ball as you move forward into a balanced finish.

Gaining feel

The standard pitch calls for about a three-quarter backswing and a follow-through of equal length. But the shorter the pitch to the green, the shorter you should make the backswing and follow-through. This is where 'feel' comes into play and this is a skill that cannot be taught easily. That's why you must practise this shot as often as possible to get the hang of it, while also fighting any tendency to decelerate the clubhead at impact.

Try hitting pitches at a variety of distances when you go to the range, picking out a target at 35 yards (32m), then 50 yards (46m), 70 yards (64m) and so on — until you can comfortably land the ball to within 'makeable' putting distance. Or set up an open umbrella — upside down, top spike into the ground — and pitch balls into that.

The more you practise this shot at different distances, the more you will overcome the fear of mishitting the shot under pressure.

TEMPO IS KEY

Varying the length

Another key to varying the length of the shot is to narrow your stance slightly for the shortest shots. This naturally cuts down on your turn, while keeping most of your weight on the left side will also help produce the desired effect.

It can also be useful to imagine a clock mounted behind you, and hit different increments on that clock face for each shot. For example, a three-quarter swing for a pitch of 85 to 100 yards (78 to 91m) might require the club to stop at about 10 or 11 o'clock on the backswing and hit the 1 to 2 o'clock mark on the follow-through. A shot of about 50 yards (46m) would mean hitting the 9 o'clock slot on the backswing and the 3 o'clock mark on the throughswing.

Tempo is the key

Even with the shortest pitches, you must be positive or you will commit a multitude of sins. Maintaining a smooth, even tempo is a key factor in the pitch shot. Despite the compactness of the swing, a steady pace is necessary to ensure that the clubhead swings firmly through the ball, just as with any other shot – but perhaps more so with the short irons.

ABOVE The length of your backswing will be the governing factor as to how far you will hit the ball. When you are practising these shots, experiment with differing lengths of backswing and note how far the ball travels.

ABOVE The length of your follow-through should mirror the length of your backswing. This will ensure you don't quit on the shot.

LEFT As with all shots, a balanced finish indicates a controlled swing and will help you gain consistency.

Finally, don't forget what I told you in Chapter 2, Preparation, regarding your pre-shot routine.

With pitch shots, it's essential to 'visualize' the shot before playing it. Pick a spot on the green and imagine the ball flying through the air, then landing softly and rolling up to the flagstick.

Now you're ready to hit a solid pitch and shave strokes off your score.

CHIPPING

Learning the basic technique of chipping could save you six strokes a round. It will not happen tomorrow, because the technique you are about to learn – like the pitch – demands a few weeks of practice. But compared to perfecting the full swing, it is easy.

When you're practising, try rolling the ball underarm towards your target. This will help you to visualize the shot rolling towards the hole.

Your first objective is to choose your weapon.

Chipping is perhaps the most humble – and yet important – stroke in the game. And even though it has often been said that you drive for show and putt for dough, few golfers consistently hit the green in the required one, two, or three strokes regularly to threaten par. However, as we get better and better, we do get closer to the greens with most shots – and that's where chipping comes into play.

Maximum feel

The chip is a stroke played anywhere from a few feet to 30 yards (27m) off the putting surface. The goal is to get the ball close enough with your chip to have a tap-in with your putter on the next shot. Along the way, you might even hole a few chips.

This is another shot that calls for a maximum of 'feel' and imagination. And that means practice, practice – and more practice.

In a nutshell

Here's how you do it. Any club from a 5-iron to the sand wedge can be used for chipping, depending on the position and lie of the ball relative to the pin, the amount of green you have to work with, and whatever ground you have to carry the ball over to get it rolling. That's the key thing. Get it rolling on the green.

As Ray Floyd, one of the finest short game players ever, said in his book *From 60 Yards In*, this shot 'is simply putting with a lofted club'. You'll see why as I describe the technique over the next few pages.

Judgment call

First, visualize your shot. If you are on the fringe of the green with, say, 30 feet (9m) to the cup, pick a spot where you want the ball to land. Take into consideration the break on the putting surface and any other factors that might come into play – such as the slope or the wind.

The key to executing this shot successfully is your ability to judge distance and how the ball will roll, just as if you were about to hit a putt. This will take some preliminary practice to get a feel for if you are a beginner, while the more experienced player will have the advantage of being able to conjure up the memory of a similar shot from the past.

A good rule of thumb is that when you use the standard chipping stroke, and strike the ball with a medium to short iron, the ball will travel about a third of the way to the target in the air and the rest of the way along the ground – depending on the situation.

Conversely if you throw the ball in the air, you inevitably find it more difficult to get the ball close to the hole.

PRO TIP

In recent years, golfers such as Tiger Woods have popularized the idea of using a 3- or 5-wood in certain situations to chip from off the green. Woods uses this club to keep the ball even lower than when chipping with an iron, reducing any risk of a bobble or bounce with the slight initial elevation on a chip shot. The key is to be confident and take an even, smooth stroke.

A FEEL SHOT

The chip shot can be played from a few feet to up to 30 yards (27m) off the putting surface. When playing the shot, your head should stay very still and your weight should favour the left foot. Feel is the essential factor when playing this shot, and feel can only be developed through practice.

THE BASIC CHIP SHOT

Now it's time to select your club. Some golfers like to use the same iron for all chip shots, and that's often a pitching wedge or a 7-iron. If you are a beginner, that's probably not a bad idea.

ABOVE Choke down on the club and ensure that your hands are ahead of the clubhead at address.

But if you have played the game for a time, you will know that each club produces a slightly different effect, and that club selection is crucial. Picking the right club – in combination with a solid chipping stroke – can make the difference between a long, difficult putt for par versus a short, easy one.

In general, the further away from the green your ball is lying, the more lofted a club you need to carry the intervening grass or hazard. The added height such clubs naturally put on the flight of the ball will also help impart the backspin needed to check the ball when it hits the green and prevent it from shooting past the hole.

Elevation and roll

If you are on the fringe – say only about a yard (1m) off the green – and the pin is about 30 feet (9m) away, a 6- or 7-iron is ideal, since it will elevate the ball onto the edge of the green, and then let it roll the remaining distance like a well-struck putt.

However, if you are about 15 feet (5m) further back, you'll probably need a wedge with enough loft

to keep the ball in the air about the same distance, and then land the ball on the green and let it roll up to the hole. Any further back than that and you would be playing, in effect, a pitch or possibly a lob shot, which will be described in later chapters.

The set-up

Now you're ready to take your set-up. The first thing is to position your feet about a foot (30cm) apart in an open stance, angling the front foot out some 20 degrees – just like you did for a pitch shot – while keeping the rest of your body and the clubhead parallel to the target line.

Now concentrate most of your weight on the front foot and position the ball towards the back of your stance, just inside the big toe of your right foot.

Choke down on the club until your lower hand is at the bottom of the grip near the shaft – you can use your putting grip (see Chapter 6, Putting) if that feels more comfortable – and push your hands ahead of the ball at address, so that you can hit the shot with a slightly descending contact.

HANDS AND LENGTH OF SWING

Take the club away with the arms and hands.

Regulate the length of swing in relation to the distance of the ball from the target.

With hands ahead of the clubhead, swing through with the left hand moving towards the target.

Brush off

Finally, in order to execute the shot, think about your putting stroke.

Keeping your hands, wrists and arms fairly passive, start the backswing with the same, smooth pendulum motion – arms forming a triangle with the shoulders as the base – that you use for putting.

As you come through the ball, just brush it off the grass, making sure your follow-through is the same length as your abbreviated backswing. And just as you do while putting, keep your head down until the ball is well on its way to the hole.

With a little bit of luck, and a solid chipping stroke, by the time you look up, the ball will be disappearing from sight and you'll be able to mark a par or birdie on your scorecard.

LEFT AND BELOW A putter is a real option when you are on the fringe of the green. Remember that the grass you are putting through should not be too thick and it must be dry.

SETTING UP A CHIP SHOT

LEFT The set-up – begin with your normal pre-shot routine: aim the club, align the body, position the ball, grip and posture.

BELOW You will be confronted with many situations where a sand or lob wedge are necessary to lift the ball over a hazard and land the ball softly.

CHIPPING WITH A WOOD

This is the 'Tiger' shot. Played from just off the green, the 3- or 5-wood can be highly effective in lifting the ball over the apron and rolling the ball towards the hole. Practice makes perfect.

5 BUNKER PLAY

The bunker shot – which strikes terror into most high handicappers – is actually the easiest shot in golf since it leaves the player the highest margin for error.

GREENSIDE BUNKER PLAY

On most weekends, my golf club is crowded with people using the driving range, playing the course or enjoying a meal or drink in the restaurant. But the area in front of the clubhouse, where we have a practice bunker and green, is usually deserted.

Now why is that? Especially since many high-handicap golfers are terrified of landing in sand traps, and, once there, are often ready to capitulate mentally. Because – assuming they will not get up and down for par – they have already resigned themselves to making bogey or worse.

Removing the mystery

In this chapter, I'll show you how to gain more confidence when you end up in sand by demonstrating what is really one of the easiest shots in the game. As with any fear or phobia, taking the mystery out of things can help to solve the problem.

For proof, ask any pro or low-handicapper whether he would rather be in a trap or in the rough, and he will tell you it's no contest. If you're going to make a mistake around the greens – and you are bound to do so during the course of any round – sand is the best place to find yourself.

From a bunker, you have a large margin of error, you can usually put some spin on the ball, and your chances of getting down in two shots should be better than 50:50.

But as with chipping and pitching, practice is fundamental to mastering this vital shot.

Preparation

The key to playing successfully from the sand is to be positive before you even step into the bunker. How many times have you left the ball in the trap once – or

Taking the fear out of bunker play comes down to practice. If you fear this shot, read the next few pages and then stay in the bunker until you believe me.

Your feet and hips should point left of the target (open stance).

Position your ball on the inside of your left heel.

Keep your weight principally on your left foot throughout your stroke.

even twice – or bladed it over the other side of the green and into more trouble?

Being afraid of this shot will paralyze your swing and stifle your momentum. And, as with most shots around the green, a smooth but crisp tempo is essential. When a golfer goes into a mini-panic, or is unduly worried, he often fails to swing through the ball, which is the cardinal sin in bunker play. Leaving the clubhead in the sand ensures the ball will stay there as well.

Shot rehearsal

Let's go back to the idea of always rehearsing a difficult shot before hitting it. In the case of bunker shots, this takes on added importance, since this is a unique shot, and it is against the rules to ground your club in the hazard before you take your bunker shot.

First, visualize the shot before getting into the sand – actually conjuring up a mental picture of how the

ABOVE Getting a feel of distance, where you will land the ball, and how the ball will fly is especially important before going into the sand, as often you may be unable to see the flag when playing from a deep bunker.

shot works (which I'll explain in a moment), then imagining the clubhead sliding into the sand, and the ball lifting up on a wedge of sand to the green and trickling towards the hole.

Second, I would suggest that you take a few practice swings outside the bunker, using the same set-up and swingpath you will use once inside. When you do go into the bunker, move your feet from side to side to give yourself a firm footing. This will also enable you to assess the depth and texture of the sand, giving you more clues on how to play the shot.

Now it's time to climb into the bunker and go for that par with confidence.

THE SAND WEDGE

In the 1930s the legendary Gene Sarazen invented the sand wedge, a club that changed the way golf was played. Before that, golfers had to improvize when they found themselves in a bunker, using a variety of clubs in a variety of ways to escape from trouble. So don't neglect to take advantage of it.

The sand wedge will always do the job in a bunker if you know how to use it, which may seem like an obvious and even laboured point. But it isn't.

Many golfers never practise this shot. As a result, when they are forced to hit out of sand, they have no idea what this unique club can do, nor how to make it do what Sarazen had in mind – even more than 70 years later.

More surprisingly, some golfers do not even carry a sand wedge in their bags. If you are one of them, remedy that situation immediately. It will save you shots and a lot of heartache out on the golf course.

Consult a PGA pro before making a purchase as choosing a sand wedge with the correct design for the conditions where you play is essential – they do vary.

The most important aspect of the bunker shot is the follow-through. Too many players stop at impact, so don't get trapped – make a big throughswing taking lots of sand.

Up and over

The sand wedge should not to be confused with the pitching wedge, although many beginners tend to mix up the two clubs.

With 56 degrees of loft, the sand wedge is designed to lift the ball upwards and impart spin, which also makes it handy on the fairway from 80 yards (73m) or less to the green. In addition, there is a wide flange on the sole of this specialized wedge that helps encourage the clubhead to slide through the sand and prevents the leading edge of the blade from digging in – what golf pros refer to as 'bounce'.

That's the reason for carrying a sand wedge, because the bunker shot is the only one in golf where we do not strike the ball directly. Instead, the golfer

BUNKER PLAY

GETTING OUT OF A RUT

A forerunner to Gene Sarazen's modern invention of the sand wedge was a variation on the mid-19th-century club known as a 'cleek' (there were also driving and even putting cleeks), which had a lofted iron blade. Used to play off tight lies and sand, the cleek was ideal for hitting out of cart tracks. In those days, especially along the links land of Scotland, the townspeople had the right of way to cart off sand, gravel and seaweed, and whatever they could salvage from items routinely washed up on shore from passing ships.

Removing sand before the ball is your safety margin that will guarantee success playing from the sand.

hits one to two inches (2.5 to 5cm) behind the ball, the clubhead passing through the sand and under the ball to lift the ball up and over the forward lip of the bunker and onto the green.

Aggressive stroke

Notice I said that the clubhead passes under the ball. In effect, it is the momentum created by a positive stroke that is transferred from the club to sand to the ball. Thus, the sand wedge allows a golfer to hit an attacking shot that imparts spin and stops the ball quickly on the green.

But how is it possible to hit aggressively, never touch the ball – and yet get it to travel only a few feet with backspin?

That's where the set-up comes into play. And once you master that, hitting the basic sand shot should become second nature.

When you're practising (you're not allowed to do this in a game), draw a line in the sand either side of the ball. Once you've hit the shot, check to make sure that all the sand was taken.

THE BASIC SAND SHOT

Assume an open stance – with feet, knees, hips and shoulders angled left of the target line – and with the clubface open to your stance line, but square to the target. The ball should be positioned in the middle of your stance, with most of your weight (about 60 per cent) resting on the front foot.

As we shall see later, depending on the height you need to achieve to clear the forward lip of the bunker, and the pin placement, these alignments will differ slightly. But, as a general rule, the more height and spin you need, the more you should open your stance and the clubface while also moving the ball further forward in your stance.

LEFT If you need extra height, open your clubface.

RIGHT Move your feet in the sand to get a firm footing.

FAR LEFT The sand wedge is shaped differently from other clubs in the set as it is made with a flange on the sole to prevent the club digging in.

LEFT Taking your stance in a bunker requires you to dig your feet in. Therefore you need to grip down the club to compensate.

FAR LEFT Sand wedges do vary in shape, some having a larger flange than others. It pays to hit some different trial sand wedges and find one that suits your game.

Digging in

Now give yourself a secure, balanced footing by digging your spikes into the sand, twisting your feet until your movement is restricted, the sand about as high as the soles of your shoes. This will also provide more clues about the texture and density of the sand.

With practice and experience, you will learn how to adjust your swing to suit different conditions. For instance, with wet, coarse sand, your ball will come out hot and fast, so you may have to shorten your swing. On the other hand, fine, powdery sand will demand more speed and a longer swing to avoid burying the clubhead.

Grip and choke

Now you are ready to grip the club. I suggest you use your normal grip, but some golfers prefer to weaken theirs for a sand shot, to ensure the clubhead stays open. If you normally use a slightly stronger grip to help avoid a slice and get more distance, I'd suggest moving to a neutral grip for bunker play to avoid any tendency to dig the clubhead into the sand.

Whatever grip you use, choke down on the club. By twisting your feet into the sand, you have shortened the distance between your hands and the ball, and, as with any shot, you will want to maintain a full extension of your left arm through impact.

Positive hit

Finally, you're ready to hover the club over a spot on the sand about an inch and a half (4cm) behind the ball, and start your backswing along the line formed by your feet – or along an out-to-in swingpath.

Break your wrists early and take the club back smoothly – good tempo is the key to any bunker shot. As for the length of swing, that will vary with the type of shot required. Consider a three-quarter backswing as about average.

As you begin your throughswing, keep in mind that the crucial element in any bunker shot is not to leave the clubhead in the sand. Hit with a positive blow, slicing through the sand to a full, finished position. If you do that, the ball will rise high out of the bunker and land softly on the green.

BUNKER PLAY

ABOVE Confidence is the key to good bunker play. Keep your tempo smooth, take sand before the ball, and follow through.

PLUGGED LIES AND LONG BUNKER SHOTS

Golf balls have a nasty habit of finding fiendish ways to plug in bunkers, and playing them from such a lie makes sand shots that much harder. But with the right approach, you can extract a ball from almost any plugged lie.

But remember – as with any shot out of the sand – you are never striking at the ball directly. Rather, you must find a way to let the club get into the sand and under the ball, then lift the ball out on a bed of sand, somewhat like blasting your way out of trouble.

With a normal lie in the sand, you can achieve both height and backspin this way. But for most plugged lies, the ball will come out low and with topspin – since you'll often be hitting it with a closed clubface – which makes it run when it lands. Try to allow for that.

LONG APPROACH BUNKER SHOT

Long bunker shots need to be played with conviction. If you are not too close to the lip of the bunker, consider using an 8- or 9-iron or a pitching wedge. Aim to nip it cleanly off the sand with a full follow-though.

Sharply down

Many plugged lies occur on the front edge of a bunker, when we come up short trying to hit a pin close to the near edge of the green. For this shot, set up as you did for a ball on an upslope, with your shoulders parallel to the slope. Square up or slightly close the clubface and hit sharply down, causing it to enter the sand just behind the ball. You may leave the club in the sand with this shot, but if struck properly the ball will pop up and might even stop quickly on the green.

For a more conventional plugged lie elsewhere in the bunker, try to hit sharply down just behind the ball with the clubface square or closed, and try to limit your throughswing so the clubhead does not pass your hands. In this case, the ball will again rise up on the sand, but roll further on the green.

Your grip pressure on all shots from plugged lies should be firmer than normal, to allow for the harder impact of the clubhead hitting into the sand.

Long bunker shots

A bunker shot of 40 yards (37m) or more is among the toughest in golf. That's because it's so hard to gauge the distance the ball must travel, regardless of its lie in the bunker or the position of the pin.

Try to play this shot as close to a normal hit off the fairway as possible, much like a pitch. First, consider the height of the lip of the bunker. If it is low enough, and the ball is sitting back far enough, you might consider using a pitching wedge, a 9-iron, or even an 8-iron if you think it will clear the edge of the hazard.

Square up the blade of your club, play the ball off your left heel, and think about nipping it cleanly off the surface of the sand. Then swing with conviction!

Given a chance

The same applies to fairway bunkers (covered in more detail in Chapter 8, Trouble Shots), where the shot might be 150 to over 200 yards (137 to over 183m). In such circumstances, if you have a favourable lie you might even try hitting a wood.

Again, the key is experience and practice. The first few times you try shots like these, the results might be near-disaster.

Remember, the first priority in hitting any bunker shot is to get out! If the ball is plugged, too close to the lip for comfort, or the rim of the trap is too high to clear, simply forget about reaching the green and go back to your sand wedge. Then try to land your ball somewhere on the fairway that will give you a good second shot, perhaps playing the ball out of the bunker sideways or even backwards. That way, you will at least give yourself a chance with your next shot.

When playing a plugged bunker shot, keep the clubface square, allow for the ball to roll on the green and hit down into the sand.

THE PLUGGED BUNKER SHOT

6 PUTTING

Putting accounts for at least 50 per cent of the game, or a possible 36 strokes taken in an even-par round of 72. Here's how to start working towards cutting your score dramatically by more effective putting.

PUTTING

Drive for show and putt for dough is, quite rightly, one of golf's best known axioms. Putting adds up to 50 per cent of the game, or 36 of the 72 strokes you might take in a round of even par.

Put another way, if you routinely miss just a handful of makeable putts per round, it will result in a major difference to your score and handicap. Instead of playing to an average of around 18 strokes over par, it puts you into the very mediocre range of the mid-20s duffer. So rather than consistently threatening – or actually scoring – in the 80s, you're going to be struggling to break 100!

Vital game

Does that sound like your game? If it does, then this chapter is for you – not to mention everyone else who currently plays the game of golf. Name the last player to win a major tournament who did not putt well. Or name a great player from any era – from Harry Vardon to Tiger Woods – who was a poor putter.

Putting is the most vital game within the game of golf, and all the great players are great putters.

Consistent stroke

Putting well demands a precise physical and mental approach that in some ways is far more difficult than any other shot in golf. As stressed throughout this book, the secret to playing well is having a 'repeatable' swing. The same holds true when you take the putter from the bag.

There is little margin for error in this phase of the game so it's really important to get the fundamentals of putting right. That means learning to strike the ball with a repeatable, smooth putting stroke. It's the best way to start really improving your scores and consistently playing well.

But putting is not just about good mechanics. You also need feel and touch, the ability to judge distance, the skill of 'reading' a green, all acquired through experience. In addition, you must bring that other, less tangible, quality to your putting game – confidence.

One of the reasons why soft spikes are often insisted upon is that metal spikes can cause marks on the green that affect the roll of the ball.

A consistent, repeatable putting stroke is just as important as a good golf swing. Time devoted to this part of your game will be well rewarded.

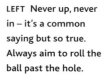

LEFT Never up, never in – it's a common saying but so true. Always aim to roll the ball past the hole.

ABOVE When lifting the ball out of the hole do so at arm's length so as to avoid unnecessary wear around the hole.

Natural outcome

The object of every putt is to hole the ball, or at least to leave the next putt within the 'gimme' range. Anything more than two putts on any green is a waste of strokes that will have a significant impact on your scorecard, and may well influence your mood on the next tee with negative consequences.

So let's work first on how to putt more successfully. Once you can do that, the natural outcome will be an increase in your confidence, which will spread to the rest of your game. Putt better, and you'll gain confidence. Gain confidence, and you'll putt better. It's a virtuous circle. In other words, if you approach every putt thinking you can make it, you're halfway there.

Bob Charles – the left-hander whom Jack Nicklaus once called one of the greatest putters ever – said that his putter was the 'life-line' to his game, and the key to every victory he ever achieved – with confidence providing the crucial link between technique and execution.

Remember, the last stroke you take on every hole is a putt, and in many cases – whether it drops in the hole or not – it's often the most significant.

THE PUTTING GRIP

Golfers use a variety of grips when they putt. Whether pro or amateur, the grips of players I teach are almost as individual as the golfer.

Some golfers simply use the grip they employ for woods and irons – be it the Vardon, interlocking or ten-finger 'baseball' grip. Others reverse the position of their hands on the club, adopting a 'cross-handed' or 'cack-handed' grip. A few even putt from the opposite side to the one they use for their normal golf swing. In addition, there is the question of how much pressure to exert in the grip. Some golfers will opt for a strong grip, while others will favour a weak or neutral grip.

The reverse overlap grip

The most common grip I see used today is the 'reverse overlap'. It's the one I prefer, and I recommend it to most of the golfers I teach.

The reverse overlap is the most fundamentally sound putting grip, and offers the average player the highest chance of success. With this grip, the hands are positioned on the club in a way that naturally binds them together as a unit, while removing any tendency to get 'wristy' in the putting motion.

In the reverse overlap, the palms are positioned in opposition to each other, which also provides stability. Combined with the proper set-up and stroke, this grip gives the golfer the best chance of keeping his putter

square – or moving it straight along the imaginary target line to propel the ball forwards on the correct line to the hole.

Assuming a grip

Here's how to assume the reverse overlap grip:
• Place your left hand against the grip handle of the putter, leaving a gap at the top of at least an inch (2.5cm). Now grip the club lightly with the middle, third and little fingers of your left hand. Keeping your forefinger off the shaft, point your thumb straight down the grip.

• Place all four fingers of your right hand on the club, aligning the grip along the pads at the base of the fingers. The little finger of the right hand should be resting snugly against the middle finger of the left hand and the right thumb should also be pointing straight down the grip handle.

• Finally, position your left forefinger in one of the three following ways:
  ❶ Around the little finger of the right hand.
  ❷ Crooked around the ring finger of the right hand – overlapping the last two fingers.
  ❸ Or run it straight down across all the fingers of the right hand.

Take time forming your putting grip. Just as in the full swing, the placement of your hands makes a big difference to your final stroke.

THE REVERSE OVERLAP PUTTING GRIP

 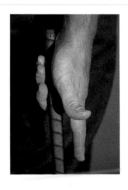   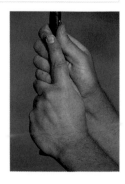

Any of the variations described in this final step will form a good reverse overlap grip. Try each one to see which suits you.

But remember, only do so when practising. Never experiment on the golf course. Any change while playing will distort your feel for the putting motion and may even pull your stroke off line.

Grip pressure

Grip pressure is a matter of individual choice.

Tom Watson, one of the best putters the game has known – even though he had problems with that aspect of his game in later years – believes in varying his grip pressure. Watson favours his left hand, so he can guide his stroke with the leading hand. He exerts more grip pressure with the last three fingers of the left hand, plus the index and middle two fingers of the right hand.

My own preference is to keep the pressure from all of the fingers and the thumbs constant throughout the stroke. I like to hold the club firmly, and yet lightly, in much the same way that I recommend you to grip woods and irons.

Focusing guide

When I'm having trouble with my putting, I often try to focus on my left hand for a time, in effect just slightly tightening my grip pressure with that hand in an effort to use it as a guide in stroking the putter towards the hole. I think about keeping it firm throughout the stroke.

As ever, consistency is the key.

Experiment with every possible variation in your grip pressure on the practice green. But when putting on the course, make sure you maintain the same pressure throughout the stroke.

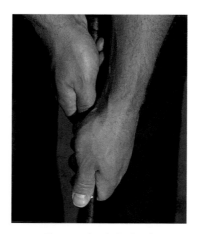

ABOVE The cross-handed grip, where the left hand is below the right hand, is worth trying.

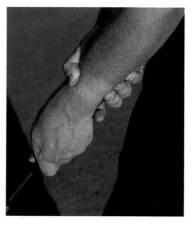

ABOVE The Langer grip, developed by Bernhard and used to great effect. Only try it if you're desperate!

PUTTING YIPS

Some golfers, especially pros and those with more experience, develop the 'putting yips' – a vague, anxiety-related condition that causes a player to stroke across the ball with a short, jerky stab. Often, a golfer can't pinpoint when the problem first occurred. But such famous players as Ben Hogan, Tom Watson and Bernhard Langer have known the agony of suffering through the yips at one or more points during their careers. There's no absolute cure for the yips, because the problem is often psychological and far too complex to analyze. However, overcoming the yips is possible, as both Watson and Langer can attest.

The first step to a cure is to experiment with several options, at least for a time. The cross-handed grip – reversing the position of the left and right hand on the putter – that Fred Couples has used is worth trying. A broom-handle putter has also helped Langer and Sam Torrance. Simply consider any method you choose as a way of getting back to some form of normality and regaining confidence. Keep in mind as well that the yips can come from being too intense over the ball, much like the idea of 'keeping the head still' during the golf swing. Discipline yourself to take one look and then hit. Spending too much time over the ball causes you to freeze up, and then you will barely be able to move, which can lead to a very jagged and irregular stroke. Trust your instincts and try to keep it short and sweet.

Finally, when you're practising before a round, instead of hitting long putts focus on several short ones. Putting the ball into the hole is the best way to cure the yips, and the yips tend to affect the short putts more than the long ones. Tom Watson had most problems with three- to four-foot putts, and the majority of golfers suffer from the same problem, finding it easier to deal with a 40-foot (12m) putt than a crucial short one.

THE PUTTING SET-UP

The putting stance is another area where golfers display their individuality. Some set up slightly open to the ball, while others use a closed stance. Some bend low, and some stand almost straight up. The arms may be tucked in or flared out. The feet may be close together or spread wider than shoulder-width.

Why all the differences? Because of two factors common to all putting styles. First, when putting, every golfer tries to get as comfortable over the ball as possible – which ought to breed the confidence needed to make the putt. Second, they are trying to position their eyes directly over or just inside the ball-to-target line.

Eyes lined up

There is no disputing the fact that unless your eyes are lined up above the ball or just inside it, it's extremely difficult to stroke the ball successfully on a line to the hole. In the case of right-handers, this means the left eye specifically. If your eyes are lined up outside the ball, you will get a distorted view of the target line and will probably pull the putter back on an outside path, which may result in a putt missed to the left.

Everything square

So how do you position yourself to make most putts? I'm all for being comfortable over the ball, but unless you can claim almost flawless success with your current set-up position, try – at least for a time – the classic method described below.

In watching golfers such as Bob Charles, Ben Crenshaw, Tiger Woods and José-Maria Olazabal over the years, I have become convinced that the best putting stances are those where everything is absolutely square to the ball and line of putt – feet, knees, hips and shoulders. The ball is forward of mid-stance – or inside the left instep – and the eyes are directly over it, with the arms hanging naturally, forming an almost perfect triangle with the shoulders.

From this position, these pros seem to move the putter effortlessly – first back, and then through the ball – in a rhythmic, pendulum motion. The result? They sink more than their share of putts to capture the big tournaments.

Winning formula

Here's how to assume that winning formula in your set-up:
• Positioning the ball inside your left heel, set yourself so that your left eye is directly over the ball. You can test this by dropping a ball down the sight line of your left eye. If you are lined up correctly, that ball will hit the ball on the ground below you.
• Now try to get comfortable by letting your arms hang naturally, flexing your knees and bending forwards from the hips. Wiggle your toes inside your shoes until you balance your weight evenly between both feet – with your feet set at a distance of about 12 inches (30cm) apart.
• Finally, align your body – shoulders, hips and feet – parallel to the line of the putt.

When I practise my stroke, I choose a flat putt and set up guide lines as shown above.

PUTTING IN A STIFF BREEZE

I always widen my stance – and even crouch a bit – when putting in a stiff wind to gain more stability. If you were taking a full swing with this set-up, it would restrict your turn. But since you're putting, you want to minimize any body motion and anchor yourself against swaying off the ball.

By the way, don't underestimate the effect of the wind on the line of your putt. A stiff crosswind can blow a slowly turning putt off line by several inches. That's why I always recommend that new golfers hire a caddie when playing links courses, where the wind can be especially tricky. A caddie's advice on how a putt will break in the wind can save you several strokes per round.

THE PUTTING SET-UP

Alignment of the clubhead is always rule number one – take time to line up your leading edge.

Now ensure your shoulders, hips and feet are parallel to the ball-to-target line, with the ball inside your left heel.

Now you are in position, place your left hand on the club, taking time to position the hand correctly.

Finally complete putting your hands on the club in your chosen grip.

ABOVE Your left eye should be directly above the golf ball – if you drop a ball from your left eye, it should land on the ball below.

THE PUTTING STROKE

The basic putting stroke is like the motion of a pendulum, with the hands, arms and shoulders moving as one unit. There is no body rotation – the shoulders simply move back and forth. That's why it is important to align yourself correctly at address.

BELOW AND RIGHT Keep your arms, hands and shoulders working together. Your putter should be low to the ground – your head must remain very still.

Always accelerate through the ball. Your hands should remain passive throughout – and keep your head still.

As you swing the putter forward, allow the left shoulder to rise slightly – keep smooth and listen for the ball to drop. Remember, don't look up too early.

The putting stroke is another area where many golfers use highly individualistic approaches. Some are very wristy, some jab at the ball and some even hook it across the target line.

I recommend using the pendulum motion as it reduces any variables and takes your hands out of the game – which, as we have seen from the driver to the sand wedge, increases the chance of a properly executed shot.

In modern golf the hands serve as a conduit, not as the beginning and end of the swing. The pendulum motion is a long, sweeping action that strokes the ball with topspin towards the hole. Because the hands are passive and work together, the tendency to hit or flick at the ball is greatly reduced.

Low and slow

Here's how it works. Take the putter back with your hands, arms and shoulders working together – firmly but without rigidity – the length of the backstroke dictated by the length of the putt.

DEVELOPING THE STROKE

The clubhead should come back low and slow, just above the ground, and appear to be moving in a straight line – although it will in fact eventually move slightly inside the line on longer swings.

Follow the same swingpath into impact – letting the clubhead naturally accelerate from the motion of the swing – until your left shoulder rises slightly and the throughswing is equal in length to the backswing.

The overall feeling should be one of pace, fluidity and rhythm. Never force the pace, or you'll knock the putt off line. Hang onto the idea that you are stroking through the ball, not hitting it.

Anxious looks

Many golfers almost complete the putting stroke in fine style, but then look up too quickly, anxious to see how their ball is doing. If you do that, you will miss the putt more often than not. It's like failing to reach a good follow-through position on a shot with a longer club. Injecting a note of anxiety into any golf stroke, especially before completion, will lead to problems.

Never look up until well after striking the ball. This stops your head from lifting or turning. When you raise your head too soon, or too abruptly, you can cause your shoulders to move and so send your putt off the target line.

PRO TIP

The great American pro Sam Snead had the classic cure for raising your head too soon after the putting stroke. He advised golfers to listen for the sound of the ball plopping into the hole before they looked up. For those who just cannot wait that long, I recommend at least counting to two before allowing your curiosity to get the better of you.

PRACTICE TIPS

ABOVE When practising, roll a ball underarm across the green. This will help you to judge distance and pace more accurately.

ABOVE Practising putting to a tee makes the hole on the course look huge.

LEFT A miniature slice – the ball will spin right if you swing out-to-in.

LEFT Allowing the wrists to flex in the putting stroke is generally disastrous.

ABOVE Trapping an object between your arms can help to keep arms, hands and shoulders working together as a unit.

ABOVE Practise your putting whenever and wherever you get the opportunity – even in the bedroom!

THE PRE-SHOT ROUTINE FOR PUTTS

Having a consistent pre-shot routine is one of the most important aspects of putting. It should be repetitive, so that each time you step up to a putt you do exactly the same thing before striking the ball. This is vital to both your mental and physical preparation – and thus is the key to holing more putts.

ABOVE **Stand to the side – between the hole and the ball – to help estimate the distance of the putt.**

ABOVE **Always go to the lower side of the hole to help establish the line of a putt.**

ABOVE **Mark and clean the ball, then replace it with any useful markings on it parallel to the target line.**

Watch the professionals. Their routine never varies. And when they are distracted and forced to back off a putt, they always go back to the beginning of their pre-shot routine, doing the same thing over and over.

Steady aim

The first thing I do in my putting routine is to walk behind my ball and study the line that I think the putt will take – I'll explain about how to decide on the line and how to read the green in the next sections. I can usually get the best perspective on that line by squatting down on my haunches.

Then I approach the ball. Standing to the side of my line and setting the putter down, I aim the face parallel to the target line. Finally, I set my body, aligning my hands, arms and shoulders square to the line and the head of the putter.

Notice I said aim the putter first, then align the body. Doing the reverse virtually guarantees that I will be out of sync with my target and miss the putt.

Line and pace

Now it's time to take a practice stroke or two along – or rather parallel to – the intended line, not at the target. If I were to aim directly at the target, I'd be setting myself up to hit right of the hole later when I address the ball.

The number of practice strokes is up to you, but my advice is not to overdo it – one or two is about right. Each stroke should be a mini-rehearsal for the real thing. I'm trying to get a feel for the pace, or speed, of my putt, and to groove my actual stroke.

Finally, I step up to the ball, keeping everything lined up by sliding the putter forward without changing its alignment and moving both feet up an equal amount. Now, with the putter blade right behind the ball, I look down the target line towards the hole, this time trying to assess only the pace – the speed at which I will hit the ball – rather than the line.

I might check the line once or twice, but the absolute rule of thumb here is to swivel the head when doing so – rather than lifting or turning it. If I do the latter, I lose the visual sight line and may even affect the alignment of my body and/or the putter.

Deadly freeze

Once I'm positioned over the ball, and confident my overall set-up is correct, I start my stroke.

Don't hesitate here. Freezing over the golf ball is as deadly as doing the same thing over a tee shot. Tension starts to creep into the hands and arms, and the result – even at the short distance of a putt – is always a shot that goes off line.

So trust your preparation – or pre-shot routine – and let her go.

RIGHT AND BELOW When standing over the ball in the final moments of preparation, ensure that you stay loose and keep focused on a mental image of the ball rolling into the hole.

RIGHT TOP TO BOTTOM Once you've decided what you are going to do with the putt, don't waste time as this will often cause confusion and doubt, as well as being annoying for your playing partners. Take aim and fire!

READING THE GREEN

From the moment you hit a shot into the green, start to size up how you will go about sinking the putt. As you walk up the fairway, try to judge the slope and the general lie of the land.

Is the green on flat land, or part of a ridge that falls away from a hill? Is there water nearby, and do the natural contours lead in that direction? If it has been raining heavily, which way does the land drain?

Once you get closer, start to analyze the slopes on the green itself, plus the colour and coarseness of the grass to gauge the speed of the green. On hot summer days, or in warmer climates, the time of day might offer a clue about that speed. The later it is in the afternoon, given such conditions, the longer the grass and possibly the heavier the air will be, which will slow a putt down.

Finally, unless you are putting first, spend any free time practising your stroke. Then watch how others hit their putts. If you can, walk around as much of the green as possible – without causing any delay to partners or the golfers behind – getting more of a feel for the texture and grade of the putting surface.

Speed, slope and run

Everything described above amounts to a method for judging the speed, slope and run of the green – information vital to making a putt. Those are the three key words in learning how to read greens, and becoming a good putter – speed, slope and run.

Picture gallery

Before you can hope to lower your scores significantly, you have to put in the time on the practice range. This is certainly true of putting above all else.

By the time that you reach any green during play, you should have logged countless hours hitting putts uphill and down, along left-to-right breaks or vice-versa, and on slow, fast, wet or windy surfaces.

That way, once you take the first look at your putt in any circumstance, you'll have some experience to

Reading a green is an art in itself. But there can be no doubt that if you can read the slopes on a green, you will hole many more putts. If you can visualize how water would flow on a slope, that's how the ball will roll too.

fall back on. You will have compiled that mental picture gallery referred to in previous chapters – although that's only half the battle. Here's how to handle the other half.

First glance

How much will your putt break? If at all.

All three factors – speed, slope and run – could come into play here, so start by squatting behind your ball and taking a visual cue. You can also walk to the hole and try to visualize the line from there back to the ball. Returning from the hole to the ball will also help you to get a sense of what lies between, not to mention allowing you to pause to look at the putt from the side.

Once you have a sense of how far the ball will break, overplay that break. One of the most common errors I see is golfers who underread breaks. At least if you overread the break, you still have a chance to get the ball in the hole, since you will be coming in from the high side of the hole, rather than the low one – where you have no chance.

What do I mean by this? Consider a putt that breaks from right to left. That means the slope rises from left to right, or falls from right to left, depending on how you wish to view it. Thus, overestimating the break will probably put you above the hole when the putt starts to die, with a chance that the ball can still fall into the cup.

Underhit this putt and you end up below the hole, falling away down the slope.

Last turn

Next, consider the speed. The ball will break more on fast greens than on slow ones, because there is less friction to slow it down. So play more break on a fast green, and watch how the ball starts to curve more as it dies near the hole.

Of course, if you are putting downhill, there will be even more speed and break.

In the above example, you should always try to hit the ball past the hole, even if that prospect frightens the life out of you. Above all, don't be so tentative that you freeze and stab at your stroke. And don't try to finesse this type of putt, hoping it will die into the cup on the last roll. Even if you run well past the hole, you'll at least have a simpler uphill putt coming back.

Distance dictates

When playing uphill putts, you must tell yourself to hit the ball harder.

That is often quite difficult, and is rather similar to going from playing on fast greens to slow ones. Often, some mental or physical inhibition just will not let us loosen up in these situations, and some golfers consistently leave such putts short.

So again, try to visualize hitting the ball past the hole, or charging it. Of course, by that I do not mean hammering the ball. Always putt with a smooth,

BELOW LEFT Visualize the roll of the ball before playing the shot.

BELOW CENTRE Always aim to get the ball past the hole – don't leave it short.

BELOW RIGHT With long putts speed is so important – try to get the ball inside a 3ft (1m) circle around the hole.

USING VISUAL AIDS TO LINE UP A PUTT

What are the professionals doing when they mark their ball, crouch down, and then seem to fiddle with the ball before placing it back on the green? Many times, they're trying to line up the manufacturer's name with the target line to the hole. This visual aid can help both in aiming your putter blade correctly and instilling confidence, since you are giving yourself a specific cue that's easy to focus upon. Just imagine the ball rolling end over end – with the manufacturer's name holding steady at the equator – down the line to the hole. Another way of using the maker's name is to place it at the back of the ball, where the putter blade will strike first. Again, this gives you something to aim at and a way of concentrating on bringing the putter into the ball cleanly, before sweeping it away. It's easy to let your concentration drift when putting, especially if you lack confidence on the greens. Using either of these methods will get you into a sharper frame of mind and thinking about a positive result.

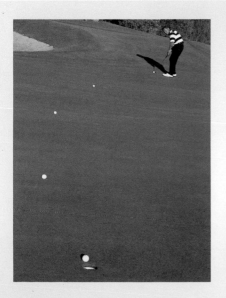

rhythmic stroke, letting the length of the putt dictate the distance the ball travels.

I find that the best way to overcome this problem is to concentrate on my follow-through. Think about stroking the putter fluidly towards the hole and the rest will fall into place.

Colourful clue

Finally, consider the grain, or the direction in which the grass lies, on the green. The longer and thicker it is, the more it will affect your putt.

How does grain affect your play? A putt hit downgrain will run faster and further than one hit upgrain. And if the grain runs across the line of your putt, the ball will break more in the direction the grain is running, and less so the other way.

You can tell which way the grain is running by its colour. If it looks light or has a sheen, you are looking down the grain, as opposed to upgrain, where the grass will appear darker and coarser.

Another way to determine the grain is to examine a golf hole. If one edge looks slightly frayed, with the ends of the grass projecting over the hole, that indicates the direction of the grain.

ABOVE If you're playing early in the morning, you will often see dew on the grass. If others have preceded you, they will have created marks that clearly show how the ball will move across the green. This can be very useful in judging your putt, but remember that the dew will slow the ball dramatically as the putt loses speed – so be bold with your stroke.

LEFT The colour of the grass will help you to decide how the ball will run. A shiny, light colour will indicate you're putting down the grain – a quick putt. A darker colour signifies that you're putting against the grain – a slower putt.

LINE OF PUTT

This is the real secret to putting. Despite how a putt may break, you should visualize each one as a straight line, and think about hitting it only along that straight line.

Let's say the green slopes from right to left. To compensate for this, pick a spot to the right of the hole. The line from your ball to this imaginary hole is the line of your putt. A ball hit down this line will curve with the slope and drift down to the actual hole, providing you hit it with the correct pace.

Pick your spot

That's the only tricky part. Depending on the speed of the green and the severity of the break, you have to make a judgement about how far from the actual hole you visualize your line, and then how hard you hit the ball down that line.

The beauty of this method is that all the putts you hit are straight, rather than bending, which is a hard concept to deal with mentally. Also, once you pick a spot along the line where you think the ball will begin to curve towards the hole, you've simplified things. Aim at that mark, making sure you hit the ball hard enough to reach it and then get beyond to your imaginary hole.

Of course, the rest is once again down to practice and feel. You will probably also have to consider other factors, such as uphill and downhill slopes and the grain of the grass.

Long putts

You should approach every putt with confidence. But a measure of reality is essential as well. Even the best golfers miss more than their share of putts over six feet (1.8m) in length, and once you are over the 20-feet (6m) range, the odds of making more than a handful are down to luck more than skill.

So on very long putts, think in terms of getting the putt close, rather than holing it. The important thing is to remain confident, yet sensible. Knock a good putt up to the hole, and then sink the next one. Now you've probably made par, or bogey at worst. But a three-putt is too costly, no matter how many strokes you took to get up to the green.

From over 20 feet (6m), visualize a circle around the hole of about three feet (1m) in diameter, and aim to leave the ball in that area. Thinking that way takes a great deal of pressure off your stroke, and should you make the long putt, consider it a bonus.

ABOVE Visualizing a putt can only be learned with serious practice. Every putt you hit on the practice green should be treated as if it's for the Open Championship.

CHARGE OR DIE

It is always important to know when to attack and when to defend. On sloping greens, this judgement becomes essential for success.

> **FIGHTING TENSION ON DOWNHILL PUTTS**
> A steep downhill putt can strike fear into even the most experienced of golfers. But don't let that fear turn into tension that restricts your putting stroke and guarantees you will stab at the ball, running it many feet past the hole. Try to maintain a feeling of real lightness in the hands, arms and shoulders during your pre-shot routine, then concentrate on stroking through the ball, just as you would for any putt. Any attempt to trickle the ball down to the hole by restricting your follow-through will have the opposite effect! The ball will shoot off the putter blade and fly past the hole, leaving you in three-putt territory. Simply control the speed of your putt by taking a shorter backstroke, which will automatically shorten your follow-through.

Added luxury

Deciding whether to play a charge or die comes with experience and practice. You should take a moment to consider the speed and slope of the green, your own ability with this sort of shot, and what you need – or don't need – to score.

In other words, if you need a birdie to win a hole in matchplay, or perhaps to avoid elimination from a competition, you might even charge a downhill putt. On the other hand, if you have the luxury of two putts for a win, you would probably choose to take the safe option and play the die, even on an uphill putt.

The immediate condition of the greens is also a factor in deciding whether to charge or die a putt. If a green has just been mown and is very slick, even with a slightly uphill putt you might want to play more break and die the ball into the hole.

By the same token, if the grass is long and slow, you could charge a downhill or across-the-slope putt, knowing that even if you run the ball past the hole, it won't go too far.

An uphill putt aimed at the back of the hole, struck firmly and aggressively, is known as a 'charge'. A downhill tickler, struck with a cautious but well-calculated hit, is called a 'die' putt – the idea being to roll the ball gently up to the hole so that it topples in on the last revolution.

The key differences between these two putts is how hard we hit them and the line we take in order to achieve success.

You will take a straighter line to the hole with the charge putt, so you must hit it with more authority to get it up the slope. By contrast, a die putt will take a wider berth because it is struck almost delicately, and thus has more time to come under and respond to the pull of gravity.

LEFT In putting, as in life, one has to decide when to attack and when to defend. Tiger Woods and Arnold Palmer have both been advocates of attacking the putt.

THE MENTAL SIDE

Now that you know how to execute the basic putting stroke, and how to judge distance and break, developing confidence in your putting stroke is crucial – and this starts on the practice green.

The art of building faith in your putting stroke starts on the practice green. Even if you only have a few minutes to spare before teeing off for a round, this is the place where you should spend that time.

Start by hitting only short putts of under three feet (1m), the sort that once on the course you might consider 'gimmes', and that might even be conceded to you by your playing partners. But how many times have you seen other golfers, or yourself, standing over such short putts and losing it? The knees turn to jelly, the arms and hands start twitching, and pretty soon a putt has been missed that most people could normally make in their sleep.

Positive sounds

So confine yourself to positive action before each round. Hit at least a dozen short putts, striking each ball firmly and with conviction, using your basic stroke, and listening for the sound of the ball striking the pin in the hole, or rattling into the cup. Now you can head for the course feeling decisive, the memory of each sweet putt carrying over to your game.

Trust yourself

Once on the course, trust yourself. Here is where the hours of practice, the experience, and your natural instincts should take over. Remember, the first glance you take at the line of a putt should tell you almost everything you need to know about the shot. You aren't building a bridge. You don't need a calculator to figure the angles. Feel the putt into the hole.

You can also try conjuring up a positive picture to help you prepare for the shot. Relax and imagine the

Even if you only have a few minutes before a round, use the time constructively by hitting some short putts and building confidence.

As with other types of shot, visualization is important. See the putt in your mind – and then feel it in your arms and hands.

This is a good exercise – start close to the hole, knock the putt in, and then move back to the next ball.

Learning to trust your stroke is the most important part of putting. It comes with hours of practice.

ball rolling down the line, then plopping into the cup. Visualizing a successful putt is halfway to making that putt, whereas letting negative thoughts intrude will almost guarantee you miss the putt. And the next one.

Remember, if you have played even one really decent round in your life, you know you are capable of making more putts than you miss. So go ahead. Trust your ability and strike the ball.

Perfection in golf is unattainable, but the best players know
how to correct a fault quickly.

CURING GRIP PROBLEMS

Remember that the clubhead should open and close in synchronization with the rotation of the body during the swing. In the backswing, the clubhead is gradually opening, then closing until it is square at impact – before closing completely in the follow-through.

If your hands are too far to the left on the club, as in the bottom picture, a slice will be inevitable. The correct hand position is shown at the top.

RIGHT When placing your hands on the club, ensure the back of your left hand and palm of your right hand are facing the target. This is the position to which they will naturally return.

But with too much tension in the hands, the golfer prevents the clubhead from reacting naturally to the path of the swing. As a result of this, the clubhead stays open at impact, which is why the ball will veer off to the right.

Free agents

Holding the club too tightly may also cause more immediate problems in the backswing. When the swing is initiated with the hands – rather than a synchronized movement of the hands, arms and upper torso – a rapid breakdown in the swing occurs. The upper body gets left behind, and when that happens the swing is destined to fail from the outset because there is no longer a co-ordinated movement.

What is the cure? It is essential that grip pressure remains light, so the wrists can remain free agents and work in unison with the rest of the body in the golf swing – allowing the clubhead to flow correctly through impact with the ball.

Too much tension destroys that harmony.

Faulty hands

After tension, the second major problem in the grip usually comes from the positioning of the hands on the club. The upper, or left, hand often tends to creep around to the right, while the lower, or right, hand, moves to the left.

When that happens, the hands work against one another, rather than as a solid unit.

Why does this occur? Most right-handed golfers unconsciously try to dominate and control the club with their right hand. The right forefinger and thumb can become especially influential in the player's stronger hand, working their way more and more over to the left.

Ben Hogan called the right thumb and forefinger the 'pincer' fingers. If they press in, all the tendons up to the top of the shoulder will tighten and even lock up, preventing a decent backswing. Additionally, the right arm will not fold properly as you go back, and the right arm will swing the club across the ball, producing a pull or slice.

Creeping hands

There is a tendency among many golfers for the left hand to creep to the right, or go underneath, because the grip seems more comfortable in that position. That movement, into what is known traditionally as the strong grip, is of less concern than the right hand moving over.

The more the right hand comes around the club, the more that influences the positioning of both hands, and thus the way they present the clubhead to the ball at impact. This will also influence the positioning of the arms and shoulders in the set-up.

If the right hand gradually creeps around to the left, then the right shoulder becomes more and more dominant until the shoulder is actually pulled out of the correct alignment. And the more the right shoulder moves out, the more likely the golfer is to swing from out to in.

Unfortunately, this produces a slice or pull, a common fault among most golfers.

Clap and close

To overcome this tendency, try to assume a more 'natural' grip. Simply allow your arms and hands to hang down naturally, with the back of the left hand and the palm of the right hand facing the target – as if both hands were about to clap together, saluting your excellent grip position. Then just close the hands around the club.

Any other positioning of the hands will cause some degree of artificiality in the swing. You will have to manipulate your hands to get the clubhead back square at the point of impact.

PRO TIP

Many top players now try to keep the right thumb and forefinger apart for fear of squeezing them together during the swing. This can tighten up the muscles of the arm and shoulder, so don't let that happen to you – it will overpower your swing. Instead, lay the thumb and forefinger on the shaft, but just leave them there, with a small gap between the two.

LEFT Place your hands lightly on the club. Nearly everyone who slices holds the club too tightly.

ABOVE LEFT A good grip enables you to swing back correctly.

ABOVE The strong or hooker's grip is certainly one to avoid.

LEFT A weak or slicer's grip will cause you to swing across the ball and so cause it to pull or spin off to the right.

CURING ALIGNMENT PROBLEMS

Proper alignment is crucial to developing a consistent golf swing. Unfortunately, the average golfer often sets his or her body at the target, rather than aligning it parallel to the ball-to-target line.

To check your alignment, first place a club next to the ball pointing at your target, then place two clubs either side of the ball as shown below. Now you can check all aspects of your set-up starting with your clubhead and moving on to your body. Note any differences from the way you normally set up on the course and you've found your problem.

Why does this tend to happen? It is natural to associate lining up to a target in much the same way as one would aim and fire a rifle – which is down the shoulder line, bringing along the feet and hips. This is totally wrong in golf.

When you swing a golf club, you are moving the clubhead at right angles to the ball-to-target line and the body must be parallel to that target line. Remember, it is the clubhead that hits the ball – not the body.

Pull and slice

If you get your body in the way of your swing, you will have a serious problem. With your body pointed directly at the target, it will be aligned too far to the right and you will block the clubhead from swinging through to the target.

The resulting swingpath will be out to in. Generally, the golfer who commits this fault will pull their short irons and slice their longer clubs.

Practise correctly

What is the cure for poor alignment? Practise with a purpose. When you go to the driving range, don't just set up in line with the edge of the mat or any other marker in your hitting area. Pick a defined target and align yourself properly with that. Otherwise, you will probably set up incorrectly and start practising a fault, then ingrain a bad habit in your swing.

The best way to practise correct alignment is by putting some golf clubs on the ground to help you aim correctly. Place one club behind the golf ball, pointing straight to the target. Then put another one down just to the right of that and parallel to the target line.

Now place a third club parallel to the first two, but left of the ball – or nearer your feet. Take away the club behind the ball and you are left with the proper alignment pattern indicated by the two parallel clubs.

Aiming the clubhead at right angles to both of the clubs on the ground, set your feet along the target line. Now you have a perfect set-up.

CHECKING YOUR ALIGNMENT

LEFT Your hips and shoulders need to be checked as well as your feet. They should all be running parallel to the ball-to-target line – that means that your body is pointing slightly left of your target, not at the target as most golfers believe.

On-course alignment cures

Golf course architects are very clever. When they design a hole, they often make the tee box (teeing area) point right or left of the target, towards the rough or other problem areas. In such situations, you must remember to aim across the tee, which is difficult. Fairways can also be cut to tempt you off to the right or left of the hole.

The way to overcome such problems is relatively simple. Walk behind the ball and choose a target a few inches in front of the ball. Focus on a piece of grass, a divot, a twig or anything you can find that is along the correct ball-to-target line. The same goes for putting. You should always find something in front of the ball with which to line up.

Body last

Now comes the most important part. The key to aligning properly is first to position the clubhead correctly along your chosen line, then set your body parallel to that line. Don't ever do it the other way around – don't ever line your body up first. If you do that, your body will generally be misaligned.

Finally, out on the golf course, if you are not playing in a competitive situation, you might try putting a club across your shoulders, hips or above your feet to check your alignment.

You can't spend much time on such methods during a round otherwise you'll hold up play. And, of course, any practice devices you might use on the range are strictly illegal on the golf course.

Use a short target in conjunction with the clubs you've laid down parallel to your ball-to-target line. This will show up any swing problems.

CURING PROBLEMS WITH BALL POSITION

The position of the ball in your stance is important to hitting good golf shots. If you put the ball in the wrong place relative to your set-up, you will make it difficult to achieve a decent strike.

When the ball is positioned too far forward in your stance, or even in extreme circumstances outside your left foot, it ends up pulling your shoulders around because you have to reach for the ball. The right arm now becomes extremely dominant, which will lead to a variety of problems.

Quite often, the golfer who does not place the ball in the proper position will also have a bad grip and alignment. He or she may aim to the right, then put the ball far too far forward in the stance.

Common nightmare

This can produce a nightmare scenario, though it is a common fault in golfers. Now the player is so turned around that the feet are aiming to the right, and the shoulders are aiming to the left of the target line. With everything completely out of kilter in the set-up, it now becomes impossible to make a decent golf swing. In such circumstances, the golfer will generally pull shots with the short clubs, and produce a big slice with the long clubs.

FAR LEFT A ball placed too far forward in your stance will cause you to pull or slice the shot.

LEFT If your ball is too far forward, it will often lead to a closed clubface and an out-to-in swingpath.

BOTTOM LEFT A ball placed too far back in the stance will cause the clubface to be open and an in-to-out swingpath.

BALL TOO FAR FORWARD

BALL TOO FAR BACK

Open and push

Putting the ball too far back in the stance is not such a frequent occurrence, but it does also cause numerous problems. Such a position will result in a push, or the ball flying straight to the right.

Remember that body rotation in the swing opens and closes the clubhead, so if the ball is too far back, you will hit it too early in the swing, when the clubhead is still open.

Because the club is still coming in on an inside track, you might also impart unwanted spin to the ball. If the ball is not pushed off to the right, you might well send it off to the left with a hook spin.

The cure? In the previous section on alignment, I suggested putting two clubs on the ground parallel to the ball-to-target line when you practise. This should establish you in the proper set-up position. It's also an excellent way to check for proper ball position.

Put another club behind the ball, but perpendicular to the other two clubs. That will tell you exactly where your ball is situated in your stance.

Practise this consistently, and you are halfway to achieving a proper ball position.

> **PRO TIP**
>
> I don't mind if a golfer plays every shot off the left heel (which is what Jack Nicklaus advocates) as long as he or she is relaxed with that and can place the ball properly. The more traditional way of positioning the ball works for many golfers, with the woods and long irons played off the left heel, the medium (5, 6 and 7) irons played midway between the centre and the left heel, and the short clubs (8, 9 and wedges) played from the middle of the stance. It's very much down to individual preference, and either choice is acceptable. The key is to be consistent – and always to place the ball in the proper position relative to the clubhead and body along the target line.

TOP ROW If the ball is placed too far forward in the stance, an out-to-in (slicer's) swing is likely to occur.

BOTTOM ROW If the ball is too far back in your stance, an in-to-out (hooker's) swing is likely.

CURING POSTURE PROBLEMS

Good posture is the cornerstone of an athletic golf swing. The correct posture gives your swing balance, which will enable your overall movement. But poor posture can interfere with balance, and once that happens everything else can start to go wrong.

THE ATHLETIC POSTURE

Most posture problems are caused by trying to get too close to the ball. Be bold, stand tall, bend from the hips and sit back – it's simple.

I believe your body weight should be slightly backwards of centre, towards the heels of your feet. If it isn't, and your weight moves forward of centre, it will result in an out-to-in swingpath, causing the club to cut across the ball.

When your weight moves forwards, your upper body will generally begin to sway forwards as well. If this happens, you put your body in the way of the swing, especially as you come through the ball. You are then forced to move the club further outside the normal swingpath – or further away from the body – hitting across the ball with a glancing blow that starts the ball spinning.

When you hit across the ball with an out-to-in swingpath, the most frequent result is a slice to the far right of the target with the longer clubs, and a pull with the short clubs.

Swing around

With your weight slightly back of centre, throughout the movement of the swing you want to rotate around the pivotal points of the right heel on the backswing, and the left heel on the throughswing. While doing this, you must keep the body balanced and exactly the same distance from the ball at all times. Only then can you allow the club to swing truly around you.

If you move the body either closer to the ball – or further away from it – you will lose balance, which in turn will upset everything in the swing. You will then find yourself in a different position at impact from the one you took up at address, and the swing can never be consistent. Indeed, you will find yourself struggling to compensate for your movement while trying to swing the club correctly.

Swing plane

Another way to focus on posture and balance is to think about swing plane. If the upper body's position lifts during the backswing, it creates a swing plane that is too flat. And when the upper body drops dramatically, it sets up too high a swing plane, with the arms lifting in the air, independently of the body.

Remember that swing plane is formed by the initial posture at set-up, and that the angle of the spine dictates the plane. We want the spine to stay in one place throughout the swing.

If that angle remains constant, the club can move around the body on a consistent circle. But if the spine moves up or down, it will take the arms, hands and club with it, dramatically altering the swing plane and thus the golf shot.

Mirror cure

How do you cure posture faults? One way is by using a mirror. Check your posture in this way as often as you can, examining your spinal angle from behind. Better still, capture yourself using a video camera, or get a friend or golf pro to take a look regularly. While practising this, close your eyes and try to ingrain the feeling of correct posture in your mind.

How do you know what the ideal posture is for you? That's dictated by your height and the length of your arms and clubs. The shorter player will be more upright, the taller one more bent over.

Following this sequence will help you to take up your particular posture correctly:

① Using a golf club, bend your upper body forwards from your hips – not from your waist – keeping the head high and the chin nicely clear of the chest. Try to retain the integrity of your head position vis-à-vis a reasonably straight line down to the base of your spine. When you bend forwards over the ball, you must retain that line – that's your spine angle.

② Now let the clubhead touch the ground.

③ Your weight will be somewhat forward, so you'll need to counterbalance that by sticking your bottom out. Adding a little flex to the knees will help to push your bottom out until you feel you're almost leaning against the back of a chair.

Exactly how the above moves are accomplished will vary somewhat with every player, and with every club that is used. A very tall golfer with a short club will have to stick his or her bottom out quite a bit – otherwise too much weight will remain forward. A shorter person with a long club will scarcely need to bend over at all.

ABOVE LEFT If your legs are too straight, you will have to bend forwards excessively.

ABOVE RIGHT Too much flex in your legs and you will be too erect in your upper body, causing you to top your shot.

BELOW If you struggle with your head being too low at set-up, practise keeping your head up as you bend forwards.

THE 'HEAD UP' POSITION

CURING THE SLICE

In order to cure the slice, you have to start with the set-up. Check your grip, alignment, ball position and posture. If the set-up is wrong, you cannot fix your golf swing. Generally, the swing itself is the last thing that is wrong.

But assuming you have a perfect set-up, what other factors can we look at?

One is the swingpath through the ball. That will be very influential. If you are slicing, you are swinging across the ball from out to in, imparting sideways – or clockwise – spin to the golf ball.

Do the opposite

What's the cure? Once you are reasonably sure your set-up is correct, try to do the opposite of what is causing the problem. In other words, you should try to swing along an in-to-out swingpath and make sure you are freely releasing the club.

BELOW FAR RIGHT As slicing is caused by swinging the club to the left of the target, practise swinging the club more to the right of the target.

Try only halfswings at first, in an attempt to gain a feel for that movement and establish it as your swingpath. Remember, if you are slicing, you have become used to swinging from out to in, and often you will not even realize you're doing it.

Then pick a target on the golf range, place some clubs on the ground to ensure your alignment is correct, and try to make the ball move from right to left. In other words, in order to cure your slice you are trying to do the opposite by drawing the ball.

In addition, make sure your hands are light on the grip so your wrists are free and the clubhead can release. Holding too tightly helps create a slice.

LEFT Ensure your hands are lightly placed on the grip.

RIGHT Check your ball position is not too far forward in the stance.

BAD SWING

GOOD SWING

OUT-TO-IN SWINGPATH

PRO TIP

Hit some shots from a sidehill lie, with the ball several inches above your feet. This can help you to produce a better swing plane and promotes an in-to-out swingpath.

TOP ROW It's the one I've seen so often – the out-to-in swingpath can only cause a pull or slice.

CENTRE ROW Here I demonstrate the correct swing. Note the differences at set-up, top of backswing and through the ball.

BOTTOM ROW The out-to-in swingpath illustrated in detail.

CURING THE HOOK

The hook is often the result of any number of set-up problems. Generally, it indicates that your hands have crept too much to the right, a position which is known as a strong, or hooker's, grip.

As your hands creep round, the shoulders tend to get more and more closed, until they are aiming too much to the right. When these faults occur, you might also find yourself positioning the ball too far to the back of your stance.

In this situation, it's also common for you inadvertently to open the clubface far too much. Why? As the ball begins to move more and more right to left, you become petrified of the left-hand side of the golf course, and will do anything to stay right. So you tend to open the clubface, aiming to the right of the target line.

Of course, most golfers don't realize the clubface is opening. They are probably convinced they are aiming straight, when they are actually aiming as much as 30 degrees right. Now the ball can only go right and the swingpath gets increasingly in-to-out, aggravating the tendency to hit a hook.

CHECK THE LINE OF YOUR DIVOT

One of the tell-tale signs of an excessively in-to-out golf swing will be shown in the divot you take. Look carefully at your divot after you've hit your shot. If it's pointing to the right of the target you're swinging too much in-to-out, thus causing the hook shot.

Trouble zone

If you swing in-to-out and hit the ball with the clubface square, the ball will start spinning right to left. Now the ball will start straight, and then begin to veer off to the left.

By contrast, if the ball is hit with the clubface even only slightly closed – say one or two degrees – that will produce a duck hook, or a snap hook. In this case the ball hardly gets airborne, flying very low and rapidly curling left.

As Lee Trevino says, you can talk to a fade, but you can't talk to a hook, because once the ball starts spinning low and left, it will bounce violently and spin off into trouble when it hits the ground.

Initial flight

What is the cure? Look at your set-up first, examining the grip, alignment and ball position. Then check the clubface. If it's wide open, square it up behind the ball. Finally, put some clubs on the ground to check your alignment and pick a defined target, working on the initial line of flight of the ball.

If you can get a friend to stand behind you at this point, that will be helpful. He or she can tell you if the ball is starting right, and spinning, which you will not be able to see yourself.

Using the clubs for proper alignment, work on starting the backswing in a straight line, trying to get some initial width. Then as you come through the ball, think about pulling the club through with your left arm, keeping the left arm and hand ahead of the clubhead, swinging out-to-in in a way rather like hitting a bunker shot.

In order to cure the hook, you are trying to do the opposite – you are trying to cut the ball, or move it from left to right, trying to hit a slice.

ABOVE The hooker will generally aim too far right (in an attempt to compensate for the ball going left) and then produce a flat swing with excessive hand action.

BELOW A great cure for the hook: give control to your left arm and try to cut across the ball as though you are trying to fade or slice.

On and off

Fuzzy Zoeller once said that he had the easiest job in the world striving to be a good golfer because he only suffered from one fault, and that was hooking the ball. So what he tried to do on any shot was to slice it.

But as with all hookers, they may be on form one day, and off the other. The American big-hitter John Daly is another classic example. He is long and extremely powerful, but tends to hook the ball. On a course such as St Andrews, where he won the British Open, he is relatively safe, because there's little

trouble on the left. But put him on a course with danger on the left, and he has a serious problem.

As with curing the slice, you have to attempt the opposite shot to fix a hook. Try to visualize slicing the ball. Try to start the ball to the left of the target and make it spin to the right. That's the quickest way to cure a hook.

BELOW Once again check your body alignment – so often this is the root of the problem.

CURING FAT AND SKY SHOTS

Fat shots — when you hit the ground behind the ball before making contact with the ball — are directly related to topped shots. If your head goes down, and then you fail to compensate by pulling back up on the throughswing, you will hit fat.

ABOVE Teeing the ball high will help get rid of the sky shot.

RIGHT An incorrect swingpath is the most common cause of fat or skyed shots.

Another reason for hitting fat is a dull strike on the ball, which can be attributed to swingpath. If you bring the club too much to the inside on the backswing, then return on the same inside angle in an excessively in-to-out swingpath, the clubhead will be too close to the ground as it approaches the ball. As a result, the clubhead could smack into the turf first.

If you are hitting either fat or thin shots and find it very difficult to hit the ball correctly when it's not sitting up on the fairway, then you're probably moving the club too much on an in-to-out swingpath.

Divot pattern

The cure is to put some clubs on the ground and practise the correct swingpath, trying to make the club go more in-to-in. Take a look at your divot pattern after every shot: if your divot is pointing slightly to the right, it means that you are coming too much in-to-out and will almost certainly hit the ball fat. If the ball is sitting down slightly, you will probably top it as well.

Sky shots

Skying the ball is usually caused by lifting the club early on the backswing, raising your arms straight up with poor body rotation. This produces a chopping motion as you come through. Another fault is the failure to clear the lower body — or turn the left hip — when you swing the club through.

PERFECT DIVOT
A perfect divot should point slightly to the left. That's because the divot should be struck just after you hit the ball, when the club is moving slightly back to the inside during the follow-through.

RIGHT If you sky shots regularly, keep the club low on the takeaway — this will prevent you from lifting the club and chopping into the golf ball.

Remember, the lower body must initiate the downswing. If the upper body is allowed to dominate, the club is forced to come outside the correct swingpath. Now you are slashing across the target line, which often results in the club chopping down into the ball and sending it high into the air.

It's important to identify which side of the swing is causing the problem. You'll need the help of a golf pro, a friend and/or the use of a video camera to do this.

Low and slow

What is the cure? Keep the club low and wide to the ground as you take it away, making sure the left arm and shaft of the clubhead form a line, which will promote a wide swing arc. Don't actively lift the club up with your right arm, otherwise you will chop down on the ball.

Are you balanced on the follow-through, and has your weight transferred to the left heel? If not, you may have moved first with your upper body, maybe even with your arms and hands, cutting across the ball.

Practise by trying to ingrain the idea of initiating your throughswing with the lower body, uncoiling from the ground up, first by turning your hips, then naturally letting your upper torso rotate back to the target and through to a full finish.

CURING THE SHANK

Is there a more dreaded word in golf? I will not even repeat it, except to say that this sometimes contagious mishit happens when we strike the ball with the hosel of the club, or the spot where the shaft joins the clubface. The ball will then career off wildly, usually at right angles to the target line.

The cause can often be attributed to the player standing too close to the ball, or shifting his or her weight too far forwards. But most of the time, the shank (there, I said it!) is caused by tension. The arms and hands lock up and the body takes over, with the shoulders pushing the clubhead down the wrong swingpath. Get rid of the tension at the set-up and you'll almost certainly cure the shanking.

Sharper strikes

The cure for this fault is to practise sharper strikes with your feet close together. This exercise restores timing and promotes better feel for weight transfer and the free swinging of the hands and arms.

And lastly, take a deep breath to make sure your breathing is relaxed and steady, and then lighten your grip pressure.

BELOW Practising half shots is a great way to get rid of shanking and sharpen your strike on the golf ball. Keep your hands light and allow the club to swing freely – enjoy yourself and things will improve.

PRACTISE HALF SWINGS

The shank is when the ball is struck in the heel of the golf club. The most common cause of shanking is too much tension, a head-down position at address, and standing too close to the golf ball. If you get rid of the tension at set-up and address the ball on the toe of the club you'll almost certainly cure your shanking.

The winner of every tournament occasionally has to escape from his or her share of desperate situations. This chapter shows you how to get out of trouble.

USING UTILITY WOODS IN THE ROUGH

A 7-wood is a club that can help tremendously when playing out of the rough. You may also want to try a 9-wood or even an 11-wood. A lot of women and senior players use such clubs, and many low handicap and pro golfers are also finding them useful.

In fact, a 7-wood is probably a better club for the average golfer to carry in his bag than a difficult 3-iron. Utility woods are much easier to use in all sorts of situations around the course, but especially from the rough. However, employing a wood depends on the type of lie in which you find your ball. In order to use a fairway wood from the rough, you must see some of the back of the ball. If you cannot see any ball, forget about using the wood.

RIGHT Utility woods are ideal for long shots from semi-rough.

BOTTOM RIGHT When playing from the rough, you will need to hold the club firmly to avoid the club getting snagged by the grass.

BELOW Trying to lead the club with the left hand (like playing a pitch shot) creates more of an out-to-in swing – this helps get a sharper strike in longer grass.

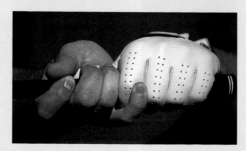

Snag proof

The reason utility woods can work out of the rough is because the clubhead is rounded, and sometimes has a V-shaped sole that will not get snagged in the grass. Also, the clubface is lofted and will elevate the ball very quickly. The quicker the ball gets up, the less it tends to fly sideways.

When using the utility woods in the rough, you should exert slightly more grip pressure than usual. You want to get down into the ball and through it, leading with your left hand.

Swingpath in the rough

Whether you use a wood or an iron from the rough, you want to swing more out-to-in, rather than the normal swingpath of in-to-in. You are trying to come at the ball from the outside, so you should take the club back slightly outside the line and pick it up a little more abruptly than with your normal swing – somewhat like a bunker shot.

Then think about trying to angle the club down, imagining you are almost hitting a slice, moving the ball from left to right as much as possible. The more you slice across the target line, the more chance you have of getting a sharp strike on the back of the ball, which will get it up quickly and send it flying forwards, imparting the proper flight to the ball.

Because of this swingpath, you might even get a flyer with a wood. In that case, the ball could travel as far as it would from a normal lie on the fairway. But again, it takes practice to judge these shots properly.

Practise hitting shots from the rough as much as you can. By developing confidence in your ability to deal with such shots, you will remove the panic factor from your inevitable visits to the rough.

When playing from the rough, take the club back a little outside the line – aim a little left and visualize a fade shot.

At the top of the backswing, maintain your composure – all too often players panic when playing from the rough and rush into the shot.

As you swing through the ball, try to come slightly out-to-in, cutting down and across the ball.

As you swing through the ball, lead with the left hand, as though you're playing a pitch or bunker shot. This will produce a 'cutting' action ensuring a sharper strike on the ball.

Swing through the ball to a positive and athletic finish and watch your ball sail towards the green.

PRO TIP

It's essential to practise hitting balls from the rough. If you don't, once you get into the stuff on a course, you will not know what to do. You'll have no feel for the situation, and you will not be able to assess the shot and choose the right method for escaping from trouble.

Find an empty field in which to practise, or any area where the grass has not been mown. Try a variety of shots and use your sand wedge or utility wood. Another option is to use the rough on your local golf course when playing on a quiet day, or the unkept areas around the practice grounds. Since they are often not maintained, the club probably will not mind you doing this. But it pays to ask first.

FAIRWAY BUNKERS

Fairway bunkers vary from the deep pot bunkers found on Scottish links to the generally shallow ones that dot municipal courses. When you land in one, the first thing to do is to assess how high the bank is in front of you, and how close you are to it.

When playing from a fairway bunker, look at the top of the ball. Grip down the club slightly and consider only a club that has enough loft to clear the top of the bunker.

Then you can decide how prudent it might be to go for a distance shot, or alternatively just take your medicine and simply try to get out, using whatever escape route is open.

Avoiding trouble

The first rule with pot bunkers is to avoid them. Generally, they are almost invisible, often hidden from view when you are standing on the tee. The land may even slope towards them, drawing the ball in.

So look at a 'course planner' (a booklet providing detailed plans of the individual holes) before you play. Try to establish where the bunkers are and how far away they are placed, taking into consideration the distance you hit a driver or other club off the tee. For example, if there is a pot bunker some 230 yards (210m) from the tee, it might well be better to use a club that you can only hit about 215 yards (197m) to ensure that you don't reach the sand.

Then you are safe even if you mishit the ball to the left or right of the fairway. For the average golfer, it just does not make sense to take on a fairway bunker like the pros do. If you end up rolling in, you will face a very tricky second shot.

Damage limitation

So you've landed in trouble. Your priority now should be one of damage limitation. Keep a cool head rather than immediately trying something heroic out of a combination of frustration and desperation.

How high is the bank of the bunker? How far is the ball from the lip? What is the lie like? Once you've answered these questions, choose a club with enough loft to get you out of the bunker — even if that means sacrificing a bit of distance.

ABOVE AND BELOW I'm using a 5-iron above as I'm a little further back in the bunker, compared to the situation below where I'm closer to the bank and so a 7-iron must be used to clear the front lip.

USING A 5-WOOD

From many fairway bunkers a shallow lip will allow you to hit the shot with anything up to a 5-wood.

BELOW Always play a club that you know will get the ball over the front of the bunker.

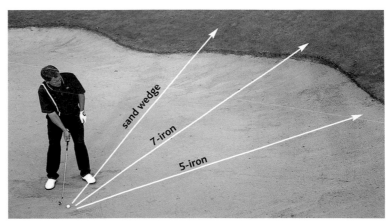

USING A SAND WEDGE

LEFT Even if you have to use a sand wedge, give careful consideration to where you want to play the ball on the fairway for your next shot – you may still make your par.

USING A LOB WEDGE FROM A GREENSIDE BUNKER

When you have to get the ball up quickly from a bunker, you might consider using a lob wedge, which many players now carry in their bags. The lob wedge can have 60 to 64 degrees of loft, whereas a sand wedge only has 56 degrees of loft.

For most golfers, the best aspect is that you do not have to open the face of a lob wedge, which is the whole reason for owning one. A lob wedge can be used with the clubface sitting squarely, which makes it much easier to play through the ball. That can take a lot of pressure off a golfer who already has enough to worry about in a bunker.

More lift

Although you can open up a lob wedge for even more lift on the ball, generally I would not recommend doing that as you risk hitting clean under the ball, leaving the ball in the bunker. So take a conventional bunker set-up with the lob wedge, then play the shot with a square clubface, aiming the blade along the line of flight – while making sure you pull the club through the sand, moving forwards rather than down.

Lob wedge versus sand wedge

Why use a sand wedge if you now own a lob wedge?

A lob wedge generally doesn't have much of a flange on it – the thicker sole under a sand iron that is angled slightly to give the club bounce and which keeps it from burying itself in the sand.

A lob wedge can have a sharper soleplate, but it certainly will not have the reverse angle of a sand wedge. The sand iron is designed so that the back of the sole sits on the ground, while the front edge is actually in the air, by as much as 20 degrees.

That is what gives the sand wedge bounce. It is made that way so the back edge will hit the sand and not dig in. In effect, the bounce stops the club from burying itself in the sand, which causes the club to decelerate or even to stop.

Different techniiques

If you use a lob wedge, keep the differences between the two clubs in mind. With a sand wedge, you can really splash into the bunker knowing that the bounce on the bottom of the club will help it keep moving. But with a lob wedge, the club may stop.

In fact, the lob wedge may just go downwards into the sand and sink in. As a result, make sure you drive through the sand more, moving forwards rather than down. Of course, you should still take some sand. Trying to hit too cleanly opens you up to the risk of thinning or semi-topping the ball.

Trust your lob wedge and swing forwards toward your intended target.

A lob wedge can have up to 64 degrees of loft – it is, therefore, ideal when you have to get the ball up quickly and land it softly.

A sand wedge can be used to play a very high shot but will need to be opened, making the shot more difficult.

Start by taking the club back outside the ball-to-target line.

Make a full backswing.

As you swing through, bring the club across the ball swinging left.

Keep the hands ahead of the clubhead as the club swings through the ball.

Make sure you swing all the way through to a complete finish.

GETTING OUT OF FAIRWAY BUNKERS

The standard fairway bunker generally has a much lower lip than a pot bunker, rising to perhaps only four feet (1.2m). However, that is intimidating enough if you are the least bit unsure about how to execute this shot.

The problem is that you have to get the ball out cleanly, but all the time you are probably thinking that you still have a considerable distance to go before landing it on the green.

So take a deep breath and try to assess what you can and cannot do given your situation. Once you've done that, try to conjure up a picture of a successful shot flying out of the bunker, then go for it.

> **PRO TIP**
>
> Since you can never ground a club in a bunker, it's a good idea to practise the technique you will use for this shot – and you do not even have to be in a bunker to do so. At the driving range, simply hold the club off the mat in the same way you would in the bunker and practise your strike, hovering the clubhead off the ground, then swinging and hitting the ball. You will quickly get used to making a good shot this way, and when you find yourself in a bunker, you will not be in such unfamiliar territory.

ASSESSING THE LIE

Assess the lie before choosing your golf club. If the ball is sitting down in the sand, you will need to use a lofted club to get the ball out.

Sizing up the lip

The first factor to take into consideration when you find yourself in a fairway bunker is how close you are to the front part of the bunker, or the lip.

If you are only a few feet away from the front of the bunker, that will have a big influence on the shot as your prime concern will be to ensure that you clear the lip with your shot – the cardinal sin is to leave yourself in the bunker. So you may have to settle for a lofted club.

If, on the other hand, you are in a position towards the back of the bunker, that can almost take the face of the bunker out of play. In such circumstances you might even be able to use a 3-wood or 5-wood to achieve maximum distance.

Assessing the lie

The second factor to consider in fairway bunkers is the lie. This is a shot where you need to make clean contact with the ball. If the ball is plugged in the sand in any way, clean contact with the ball will be impossible. So take a sand wedge, play the ball out safe, and don't expect too much.

However, if you have a decent lie and some clearance, you might consider using a wood and going for the green.

Clearing the face

When the lip of a fairway bunker is a factor, you want to choose a golf club that has sufficient loft on it, both to get the ball out and to cover the appropriate distance – without changing your golf swing.

Tinkering with your swing puts you in unfamiliar territory, which is double trouble when you are already stranded in a fairway bunker. Performing a normal swing is difficult enough.

CHOOSING THE ANGLE

BELOW When I play a fairway bunker shot, I do the following: take aim, (open my clubface if necessary), embed my feet, make a three-quarter swing and look at the top of the ball – and then off you go.

LEFT AND ABOVE A trick to help get the ball up quickly, while still getting distance, is to take a lower number iron or wood and open the face. Aim left to compensate, otherwise the ball will end up in the rough on the right.

FAIRWAY BUNKER SHOT

Extra distance and height

How do you solve this dilemma? Let's say you have a shot that demands the distance of a 7-iron, but the height of a 9.

To get the extra distance and height, try aiming to the left of the target, then open the clubface slightly and play the shot with a slight fade or even a small slice. This will produce a more lofted shot – but using your normal swing.

You should also try to focus on the top of the ball to avoid hitting it fat. And you should make sure that you have a decent footing in the sand, with your feet embedded so that you don't slip.

Using a three-quarter to full swing, try to ensure you get clean contact. Hitting the sand first will kill the shot.

Reality check

Above all, don't be over-ambitious. If you choose a club with which it is almost impossible to get the appropriate lift, the ball will hit the face of the bunker and come back at you.

Then you really are in serious trouble.

USING UTILITY WOODS FROM A FAIRWAY BUNKER

If you are far enough back in a fairway bunker to play a shot without the lip of the bunker being a major consideration, and you have a decent lie, you might consider using a wood.

In this situation, the biggest danger is actually hitting fat, which will kill any chance of either getting out or achieving any distance.

Utility woods are ideal for this shot, although you can even hit a 3-wood if you feel confident enough with that club. But I would recommend most golfers to use a 5-, 7- or 9-wood.

Any of these clubs will give you the combination of distance and a clean strike that will help get you out of trouble and perhaps even save par.

Big help

Most golfers are surprised when told that any wood is easier to hit in a fairway bunker than an iron. When you play a wood, its broad sole is a big help. Even if you do hit the sand behind the ball, the wood cannot dig in – unless you have a major swing fault.

With the proper swing applied, the wood has to keep moving, and it will keep moving forwards across the surface of sand.

Play your normal swing from a fairway bunker with a utility wood and you'll be amazed just how successful you will become at playing this shot.

General guidelines

❶ The initial weighing up of the shot is crucial.

❷ Knowing which club you are going to use and how much height you can get on the ball with it is absolutely essential.

❸ If you need to do anything different, such as trying to slice the ball slightly, be absolutely sure you know how you are going to do it – and then you must believe in the shot.

❹ Use your common sense with regard to where you are going to land the ball if you decide that you cannot reach the green.

❺ As with every shot you take, you should try to land the shot in a spot that makes the next shot as easy and straightforward as possible.

❻ The worst thing you can do from a fairway bunker is to be over-ambitious and force the shot. That's dicing with death, and a guarantee that you will soon be playing another equally or even more demanding shot from roughly the same spot.

IT'S EASIER THAN YOU THINK

LEFT Give careful consideration to where you will place your shot – here I'm going to play the ball out to the left and curl the ball with a slight fade back to the middle of the fairway. This will keep me away from the trouble on the right.

The shape of a utility wood (especially the large sole) makes playing a lofted wood easier than a long iron.

Make sure you don't touch the sand at address or on the way back – otherwise you will incur a two-stroke penalty.

As with all fairway bunker shots, look at the top of the ball in order to ensure a clean strike.

LEFT Weighing up the shot is crucial – are you far enough back in the bunker to take the lip out of play?

PRO TIP

Do not forget the rules that apply to bunker play:

- Do not ground the club before hitting the ball.
- Do not touch the sand or the back lip of the bunker on the backswing. That goes for practice swings too.
- If you hit the ball and it does not get out of the bunker, do not try to be overly courteous by brushing out your footprints or raking the bunker before hitting your second shot. The ball is still in the bunker, and therefore you cannot disturb the surface of the sand until you have hit it out.

All of the above rules carry a two-shot penalty if they are broken so it's worth knowing them.

SHORT APPROACH FROM A DIVOT

Hitting a good shot only to find that you've landed in a divot happens to everybody. So learn to cope with the frustration and deal with the situation positively.

RIGHT Playing from a divot isn't the easiest shot in golf, but if you use a lofted club, it need not become a disaster. The important thing to remember is to take a divot.

When playing out of a divot, you are trying to get your clubhead down into the divot hole, making as clean a contact with the ball as possible. Therefore club selection is all-important – although distance is not the only factor.

You are most likely to land in a divot within 100 yards (91m) of the green. But you have a problem if the ball is sitting down in the divot and a sand wedge is the right club for the distance to the green. The sand wedge is designed to bounce, rather than go down into a hole, so avoid it or you'll end up thinning the ball.

Playing with a lob wedge

The lob wedge is a good choice for an approach shot from a divot. Position the ball back in your stance and close the face a bit. That will in effect turn your lob wedge into a sand wedge, giving you loft without the bounce, helping you get the club down into the divot.

Keeping your hands fairly forward, favour your front foot with most of your weight, then concentrate on driving through the shot. Use a three-quarter swing for a more compact movement, which will help you to drive through the ball and downwards into the shot.

Downwards is important because if the club sweeps across the surface of the fairway, you will top or thin the shot. The key to this shot is to drive down into the ball with a sharp descending blow and take another divot – if you are playing from a divot, you have to take another divot.

Margin for error

The ball can shoot out of divots and take off or it can fly normally. So if there is an option in terms of where to land the ball on the green, aim at the broadest open area rather than taking the tightest line, such as over a bunker, to a small landing area. You want plenty of space to give yourself a margin for error.

Besides the lob wedge, and depending on the situation, you might also consider playing an 8, 9 or pitching wedge, none of which have any bounce on the sole. But stay away from the sand wedge!

TURNING A DISAPPOINTMENT INTO A SUCCESS

LEFT I set up with my hands more forward of the clubhead than usual. I keep a little more weight towards my left foot on the backswing and try to take another divot on my throughswing. This helps me dig down and get under the ball. And finally I drive through the ball towards my target.

LONG APPROACH FROM A DIVOT

When you are playing from a divot and need distance, don't think of using a 3- or 4-iron – in fact, avoid all long irons. Try instead a utility wood, especially if you have one with a V-shaped sole.

If the sole of your favourite wood is flat, that makes things more difficult. Imagine that shape of clubhead going into the divot. With a flat sole, you are going to hit behind the ball.

Modern fairway woods have a low centre of mass, especially the ones with loft, so they can get the ball airborne quickly. You would not hit a 3-wood from a divot, and even a 5- would be ambitious, but the 7- and 9-woods with V soles are absolutely superb.

Realistic goals

Let's say you are 175 yards (160m) from the green and you don't have a utility wood. In that case, I would suggest that you only go down to a 6- or 7-iron. You won't get any more distance than usual, because you will not get a flyer playing out of a divot, so be realistic about what you can achieve.

If there are also hazards around the green, such as bunkers, trees or water, being too ambitious could put you into further misery – instead, take a 9-iron or pitching wedge and just play the ball into position.

And remember, you must take a divot to play out of a divot!

Divot etiquette

The standard practice has always been for players to replace divots. But some golf clubs are now discouraging this, finding that replaced divots do not regrow well. Many greenkeepers now prefer to put seed and soil in the divot holes at night. So avoid doubling their work by checking what the golf club's policy is when you pay your green fee.

GET OUT OF A RUT

Remember that to get out of a divot, you have to take another divot. Many golfers fail to take divots because they lack confidence and have never learned how to hit an iron with a sharp, descending blow. To build that confidence practise by putting a tee peg an inch or two in front of a ball on the practice range. Then focus on hitting down and through the tee peg.

BELOW Playing this shot requires commitment and belief. Make a compact backswing and drive through the ball with firm wrists and, most importantly, take another divot.

Aim left of the target as you are going to cut the ball out of this lie. You can do it!

DIGGING YOURSELF OUT OF TROUBLE

TIGHT LIES AND HARDPAN

Tight lies are often encountered on links and chalk-based golf courses, or others that do not have fairway irrigation systems – especially when the weather heats up.

Keeping the weight on the front foot is the key to success in playing from a tight lie.

This is how not to play the shot. Trying to scoop the ball up into the air will lead to disaster.

Here I'm playing a sand wedge off my back foot with a closed face. My hands are forward of the clubface throughout the stroke and my weight is planted firmly on my left foot. As I play the shot, I keep my hands and weight forward at all times.

Because the fairways start to dry out and the grass does not grow lush – or is very fine and mowed closely – the ball will often appear to be sitting down. Many golfers find this psychologically difficult. They become convinced that they will be unable to get under the ball and hit their normal shot and that they will top the ball as a result.

In fact, on courses where the grass is lush, the ball does sit up slightly, with some air underneath. But golfers who are used to those particular conditions should avoid the trap of thinking that they cannot hit off tighter lies.

Take, for instance, the subsoil under many links or heathland courses. This is often much softer than it appears, and hitting down and through the ball, while taking a perfectly good divot, is fairly easy and straightforward – once the golfer gets used to the idea and is convinced that it is possible.

However, the tight lie that is truly difficult is the shot played off hardpan – dry patches of earth that in the summer months can bake into almost rock-like hardness. But even this shot can be hit successfully, and with considerable backspin, if the proper set-up and swing are employed.

A ball lying on a tight lie or hardpan is most golfers' nightmare. But if you know how to play this shot, it's easier than it looks.

Overcoming fears

The biggest problem with playing from a tight lie is often simply in the player's mind. He or she is petrified of thinning or topping the ball. As a result, this golfer tries far too hard to get under the ball, which can lead to complete disaster.

When one tries to lift the ball on purpose, there is a tendency to stay back on the right foot, then swing upwards. Doing that will ensure topping or skulling the ball. Don't change your stroke for tight lies!

You should still go slightly down into the ball. However, if you are playing on clay or chalky soil – or any other type that has become compacted in areas prone to wear – hitting too hard down into that kind of surface could injure your wrists.

PLAYING OFF HARDPAN

Landing the ball softly

I always try to analyze my shots, weighing up in my mind the different options when confronted with a particular situation. If I have a very tight lie and I'm playing an approach shot from 50 to 60 yards (46 to 55m) to the green – needing to get up and over a bunker and land the ball softly – I want to be careful that I don't get any bounce.

So if I'm using a sand wedge, I set the ball back in my stance, then take that bounce away by closing the club down and putting my hands ahead of the ball. Going through the ball, I try not to dig in too much – which will be impossible anyway – and skim the surface, keeping my hands well ahead of the clubhead and my weight very much on the left foot.

Why?

Because if the weight drifts back to the right foot, I will start to scoop at the ball.

Hardpan

Hardpan is generally hard, dry, packed mud and can be encountered anywhere on a golf course. Clay-based courses are particularly prone to hardpan, because as soon as it gets dry in the summer, the course starts to bake, the grass dies, and bare patches as hard as rock begin to form.

Hardpan can intimidate the average golfer, yet it's perfectly feasible to make a good shot off the stuff with the appropriate adjustments to your set-up, stance and ball position.

Violent check

First, put the ball back in your stance – towards the centre or even nearer the right foot – and close the clubface down slightly. On short approach shots, use a lofted club and hit down on the ball, trying your best to make a clean contact.

In fact, you can actually get more backspin on this shot than a conventional one, because – if you think about it – you have nothing between the clubface and the ball. And once you hit the ball, it will fly in quite low and bounce once, twice or three times, then suddenly check quite violently – even spinning backwards from that point.

The longer shot from hardpan

If you are playing from further away, don't make too many changes to your normal set-up and swing. I tend to put the ball further back in my stance than usual and keep my weight fractionally more on my left foot. Reducing my usual weight shift will ensure I do not scoop the ball.

Again, be sure you play through the ball, thinking about making clean contact. You don't want to hit the ground behind the ball.

I recommend that you also look at the top of the ball – as I suggested you do with the fairway bunker shot – to ensure you get clean contact.

BELOW Here I'm playing a shot off a very hard surface where my stance is also uneven. Therefore I'm limiting my weight transfer and concentrating on keeping my balance.

BELOW AND BELOW LEFT I keep my backswing smooth in order to maintain balance and help strike the ball cleanly. A three-quarter backswing is plenty here and, as with my fairway bunker shot, I focus on the top of the golf ball.

RIGHT As I've swung through the ball, I've nipped it off the surface. This shot was played to a green some 100 yards (91m) away – when the ball landed it spun back some 10 yards, which is not uncommon from this type of lie.

UPHILL LIES

Playing off an uphill lie will make the ball fly higher, and thus travel a shorter distance, so take at least one more club. Uphill lies produces a right-to-left flight, similar to a draw.

Play the ball further forward in your stance and position yourself in alignment with the slope, in this case allowing the right shoulder to drop down a bit more to mirror the rise in the land. Weight distribution will also be affected. Don't fight the slope. Simply allow more weight to settle onto your back foot.

Now aim more to the right of the target because you are going to pull the ball slightly. Don't worry about your weight transfer, which will stay a little towards the back foot.

BELOW When you are confronted with an uphill lie, allow for the ball to move left with a draw (right-to-left) flight. Aim to the right, position the ball slightly further forward in your stance and angle your shoulders so that they follow the slope you are playing from. Your weight will settle a little more towards your right foot.

Keeping balance

For any sloping lie, you must keep your balance throughout the swing. Take a few practice swings to determine how far back and through you want to bring the club. You might have to shorten your swing, using more of an arms-and-hands shot, because you will not get as much body rotation and weight transfer as you would normally.

Keeping faith

Because you will probably use more of a hands-and-arms swing for this shot – especially on the follow-through – the clubhead will tend to close. Aiming more to the right counteracts that. Execute the shot with that in mind and keep faith in the shot.

Make sure that your rhythm is very smooth. Trying to force the shot is the worst thing you can do. If you are afraid that you don't have enough club, take one more. And if you cannot do that, tell yourself that you must live with the consequences and keep it easy.

DOWNHILL LIES

Downhill lies are generally more difficult than uphill lies. Having your back foot above your front foot can feel awkward, especially at the top of the backswing, where you may tend to lose balance.

How do you compensate for the slope? The first thing to remember is that the lie will deloft the clubhead, which will mean that you will hit the ball lower and further than normal. So take at least one less club.

Then think about the effect on the spin imparted to the ball. From a downhill lie, you will generally hit the ball with a fade, or left to right. So aim more to the left and allow the ball to fade.

Do not try to fight it.

Follow the slope

In lining up, let your shoulders follow the line of the slope. Take an open stance, playing the ball further back because the club will come into contact with the ground sooner than on a level surface.

When you visualize the shot, remember that it will fly lower and have less backspin, so the ball will run further on its approach. Think about how it will land, kick and run on, and remember that it will work from left to right and kick in.

Picturing the shot always helps when playing from awkward lies. If you see a positive outcome and believe in the shot, that will go a long way towards helping you to hit it properly.

Stay balanced

The downhill lie poses more problems in terms of keeping your balance. You are definitely looking at more of a three-quarter swing, with the weight tending to stay on your front foot when you take your backswing. You should accept that you will not get much weight transfer, which will shorten your swing anyway.

The follow-through will be fairly straightforward, but make sure you do not move ahead of the ball. It's easy to allow your head to drift too far forward when playing from this type of lie. So focus on the back of the ball, otherwise you'll top it. In addition, your rhythm needs to be very smooth. If you hurry the stroke, you will lose your balance.

ABOVE Angle your shoulders to match the slope.

Place your ball further back in your stance.

> ### PRO TIP
> If you normally hit the ball with a draw, you will not suddenly hit a slice off a downhill lie – you might hit it straight. On the other hand, if you do slice or hit a fade, you might hit a massive slice from this type of lie. So take that into account.

ABOVE The downhill lie is the most difficult for most players. A three-quarter backswing with your weight staying more on your left foot is inevitable.

BALL ABOVE THE FEET

Hitting a shot when the ball is above your feet is fairly straightforward, if you are aware of a few things. The ball will definitely move from right to left, or draw. You really cannot prevent that.

ABOVE With the ball above your feet, aim more to the right of the target.

ABOVE Grip down the club to compensate for the slope.

The more acute the slope, the more the ball will move to the left from this type of lie. In fact, if you are playing from a really steep sidehill lie – with the ball perched right in front of your face – the ball will just go straight left.

Aim right and grip down

You really have to aim right, and a long way off line, to hit the ball at your target, especially with a severe lie. Also, grip down on the golf club in order to reduce the club's length. The more severe the slope, the more you'll need to grip down, otherwise you will hit straight into the ground behind the ball.

If you have to grip, say, three inches (8cm) down, that means hitting two or three more clubs than you would normally. With the worst of these lies, play a very lofted club, such as a sand wedge or a wedge, because the ball will go sideways, and the flight path could be very dramatic.

LEFT When hitting off any sidehill lie, balance is the key component to your swing, so take some practice swings.

BELOW A three-quarter back- and throughswing will help you to control this shot and hit the green with a draw.

From a more conventional sidehill lie, with the ball maybe six inches (15cm) above your feet or less, the ball will still move to the left. Depending on the way you normally hit the ball, allow for that by aiming more to the right.

Tight action

If the ball is only slightly above your feet, don't change your normal golf swing. Just keep your tempo smooth and make a clean hit. Also, you don't need to change your ball position. Just allow for the ball to go further left than usual and play your normal shot.

But if the ball is more like six or eight inches (15 to 20cm) above your feet, you have to go for a very precise strike. In this case, use a three-quarter swing, keeping your action nicely tight and compact, and making sure you get clean contact with the ball. Again, allow for the ball to go a shorter distance because you have gripped down on the club.

The key is not to try to overdo it or get too much out of the shot. Play within yourself.

The ball will draw more because you are standing more upright, which produces a flatter swing plane and causes the ball to move more right-to-left.

HOW TO PLAY THE BALL ABOVE YOUR FEET

BALL BELOW THE FEET

Playing a shot when the ball is below your feet is probably the most difficult shot for most golfers. With the ball so far down, we instinctively know that it's easy to lose our balance.

The first thing to think about when addressing the ball is keeping your weight back — or more towards the heels — and making sure it stays there. In doing this, you still must bend over sufficiently. Many players stand up far too straight, and are surprised when they top the ball. So, provide a counterbalance with your bottom. Stick it out. Sit back. Imagine you are almost sitting into the bank.

Take more club

This lie will make the ball fade left to right. It could even produce a slice. That means a loss of distance, so you need to take more club to compensate. But taking more club will also help, since added length will lessen the effect of having the ball below your feet.

When you set up, plant your weight firmly back on your heels, assume your posture close to the ball, then take a few practice swings. You have to feel comfortable with this shot, even though it's not a familiar one that you play every day.

Sense what kind of swing will work, and how much weight transfer you will realistically get — until you almost fall over. Then try to get an idea of how to play well within that range.

Stay with the shot

Do not use anything more than a three-quarter swing off a downhill lie, even if it isn't very severe — simply to ensure that you keep your balance. At the same time, make sure that you aim far enough to the left, and don't underdo it, because the ball will spin and definitely slice.

The key to success is to stay with this shot. If you come up even a fraction, you will top it. Stay relaxed, stay over the ball, use a compact swing, and believe in what you are about to do, trusting that the ball will move from left to right. And remember to stay down as long as you can.

The ball below the feet is a difficult shot for any golfer. The key to success here is being realistic in your choice of shot and then staying down for as long as you can.

BELOW At set-up keep your weight back towards your heels to maintain balance. Aim left as the ball will always fade or slice from this lie.

At the top of the backswing there is just one thing that matters – balance.

At impact concentrate on watching the club strike the ball. It's essential that you stay down with this shot, otherwise you will top the ball.

When you complete the swing, keep your balance and watch the ball fly left initially and then move right towards the target.

THE BALL BELOW THE FEET

9 ADVANCED
TECHNIQUES

Playing 18 holes of golf has been compared by some with going into battle. The more comprehensive your armoury is, the more likely the chance of success.

ADVANCED TECHNIQUES

Welcome to the master class. The term advanced techniques implies just what it says, so beginners need not apply just yet. This section is aimed at players who have mastered the basics.

Advanced techniques are, by their very definition, difficult to learn. They require plenty of practice and are even harder to execute out on the course. As a result, trying to learn these shots before you are ready could do some serious damage to your current game. In turn, that may remove your ability to score and take away all the fun from playing – a risk hardly worth taking for the beginner or even an intermediate player.

Once you have mastered the basics of the game, we can begin to broaden your repertoire of shots by playing intentional slices, hook shots, hitting the ball high and low, and much more.

Comfortable and competent

So before trying anything in this section, make sure you are already competent and comfortable with your overall golf game. In fact, check the following list first to determine if you are ready to learn the advanced techniques of golf:

• Have you have mastered the fundamentals of stance, alignment, posture and ball position, so that you can set up to the ball instinctively?

• Do you have a swing that is both reliable and repeatable – even under pressure and in high winds?

• Do you possess a solid short game – one that ensures you always get out of a bunker on the first attempt, that means you can chip and pitch well enough usually to threaten par, and that enables you consistently to sink those two-foot putts that make all the difference in your score?

It is a great advantage – when you need to create extra backspin, for instance – to have the shot in the bag. The following pages contain the information you need to play a range of golf shots you may not have even considered before.

If you didn't answer a firm 'yes' to all three items, beware of taking on any advanced technique. Doing so would be over-ambitious. On the other hand, if you think you're ready, then this section is not only essential to the development of your game but also the final path to consistent play.

Staying out of trouble

Why do you need these shots? Golf courses are designed to present a different series of challenges and to test a wide variety of shot-making ability.

Even on the first tee, you are often confronted with a situation that calls for an advanced shot. The most common challenge is a dogleg-shaped hole, which demands a ball flight from left to right or vice versa. At the same time, you may also need to shape a shot that avoids trees, bunkers, water and/or rough.

Once on the fairway, you may then have to play any number of shots that both avoid trouble and call for creative skills in order to reach the green and score well. The weather may also combine with the architecture of the course to present a host of problems and demand a series of choices.

In the last chapter, we discussed trouble shots – ways of getting out of difficult situations. If you play the advanced shots in this chapter well, you will stay out of trouble. We show you how to play shots that are slightly different from your conventional golf swing, and yet which are often demanded by golf courses and/or adverse weather conditions.

For example, if you need to play a low shot into the wind, and do not know how to play it correctly, you will probably hit the ball too high, more than likely sending it spinning off into the rough, water or sand. Then you will be in trouble and need to employ a trouble shot to salvage a bogey or worse.

In this chapter, I'll show you how to hit a draw or fade, apply backspin to the ball, execute the bump and run or lob shot, and deal with a variety of wind conditions. Knowing how to play in the wind is a key to great golf. You can use the wind to your advantage at times, but you must also know how to limit the damage when that's not possible.

So playing golf well is not only a case of having a repeatable, textbook swing. Every golfer needs a variety of shots in his or her repertoire that will allow them to adapt when the situation demands and they are called upon to raise their game.

Learning these advanced techniques is the only way to succeed in these circumstances.

Playing a dogleg or bending the ball around a tree requires some adjustments to your normal swing. These will need to be practised if you are to have the confidence to play the shot when it is needed.

Golf courses are designed in many shapes and forms with a variety of hazards. To play consistently to a low handicap you need not only to master the fundamentals of the golf swing and short game, but also to know how to cope when conditions call for something special.

THE DRAW SHOT

A draw is a shot that propels the ball from right to left. Because the ball will generally run well when it lands, it's a handy shot if you are looking to increase your length with the driver, fairway woods and long irons.

To play the draw shot, allow your hands to move slightly to the right on the grip.

The shape also helps you to avoid trouble off the tee, or play around hazards from the fairway. In addition, a draw has a lower flight path, so it's an essential shot to have in your bag for windy days.

In order to hit the draw correctly, you must swing more in-to-out than normally, and develop a feel for how to shape the shot.

Unique swingpath

How do you produce the unique swingpath of a draw? Start with your alignment, pointing your feet, hips and shoulders slightly right of the target – or in what is often referred to as a 'closed' stance. But don't overdo it. Unless you are trying to bend the ball dramatically around an obstacle, the standard draw requires that you aim right by only about five degrees.

Next, set the ball back in your stance by about an inch to an inch and a half (3 to 4cm) from where you would normally place it for the chosen club. This will encourage you to hit the ball from the inside. Finally, adjust your grip by turning your hands to the right, or more underneath the club – this is often called a 'strong' grip.

Don't overdo this as it can easily turn a draw into a hook. In fact, it's vital to experiment with various grip positions when you practise hitting a draw.

If you hit the ball with a natural fade, or tend to slice it, drawing the ball will be difficult for you. But mastering this shot can be fun. If you slice, trying to draw the ball is both challenging and rewarding, as you learn how to produce the opposite effect, which can also lead to hitting a straighter ball.

How to hit the draw

In order to encourage an in-to-out swingpath, imagine you are standing on a clockface with 12 being on the target line ahead. Aiming the club at 1, you want to take your swing back to 7, then fire through to 1.

THE DRAW SHOT

But why are you aiming at 1 o'clock rather than closing the face or squaring it to the target, which is the traditional way of teaching the draw? I believe that if you see the clubface sitting closed to your swingpath, you'll tend to swing to the left. But if you open the clubface a bit and aim at the 1 o'clock position, you are already thinking in-to-out.

I also think that a golfer should not do anything extraordinary on the backswing when learning a draw. I make a conventional backswing, then think about swinging the club from the inside on the throughswing, trying to let it drop in relatively close to my body. I promote this feeling by keeping the right elbow fairly close to the side of my torso as I start through, while visualizing how the club should swing out to the right.

Impart sidespin

It also helps to imagine you are playing this shot with a table tennis bat, attempting to impart sidespin — which in this case will be anti-clockwise. We are trying to get draw spin here, swinging the club from the inside to the outside, coming from fairly close to the body to away.

So a little extra right hand does not hurt as you come through the ball. Conjure up the idea of the right hand at the bottom of the swing arc and focus

LEFT Place the ball around an inch (2.5cm) further back in your stance.

on the impression of using a table tennis bat. Or think of it as putting forehand topspin on a tennis ball.

It is important that your hands are very free. A bit more release in the right hand than usual will not do any harm in developing the feel of a draw. But if you lock up in the hands, you'll lose confidence as you come through and block the ball to the right. This is especially important if you tend to slice.

BELOW Aim slightly right of your target and hit from 7 o'clock to 1 o'clock. Swinging out to the right will help impart draw spin and move the ball from right to left.

KEYS TO LEARNING THE DRAW

Try putting an umbrella into the ground just in front of your left foot to encourage the idea of swinging in-to-out. Now you must swing out from the right of the umbrella to avoid hitting it, and not allow the club to come back inside.

Step one – visualize the shot you intend to play.

Step two – once you've decided on the shot, commit yourself to a successful outcome. Here I'm trying to play the shot around a tree and bend the ball back to the left to hit the green.

Laying clubs on the ground is another way to groove an inside-to-out swingpath. Put one club near your feet, aiming slightly to the right of the target. Then put another club on the other side of the golf ball, pointing further right of the target. Now swing along the lines of the club next to the ball to get the feel for the correct swingpath.

Visualizing the shot

It's important to visualize any shot you are about to play, but this is particularly so for the draw. You have to see this shot in order to feel it, imagining how it will bend from right to left. But unless that flight path is very clear in your mind, you should not even attempt to play a draw.

Think of it this way. Your brain can trigger a reflex in your body, which helps develop feel for the shot. And if you can feel the proper action for making the shot, then you can impart that to your arms and hands, which will work the club across the ball – like that table tennis shot hitting the ball with sidespin.

But you also have to know where you want the ball to start. You must feel it starting out to the right, then working its way back around to the target.

I cannot emphasize that enough. You must really feel that in order to execute this shot properly, producing a movement that allows you to swing down the right path.

Remaining confident

Golfers often lose confidence in their ability to hit a draw just when they get to the top of the backswing. If that happens, they pull right across the ball and hit it way left.

Again, it's because they do not want to swing the club out to the right, which goes against their natural instincts. You must have confidence to hit the ball out to the right and then let it come back again. And only with confidence will you allow yourself to swing with a free movement.

MOVING THE BALL RIGHT-TO-LEFT AROUND AN OBSTACLE

Practising the draw

In order to learn this shot properly, you should practise first with a 5- or 6-iron. Don't use a club with any more loft than that, because the more lofted a club is, the less potential you have to put spin on the ball. That is why golfers generally hit their short irons straighter and more accurately. When the ball is going up, there's usually less sideways spin on it.

By contrast, the easiest clubs to draw (or fade) are the driver and long irons, because you can really get the ball spinning using less loft. However, you can also impart very violent spin with these clubs, so be careful not to overdo it.

Hit halfswings

Hit the 5- or 6-iron with halfswings, concentrating on the swingpath to get an idea of how to impart spin and how spin works. Again, this drill is about building a mental impression that you can transfer into the proper body movements.

Focus on your right hand, and how it has to work through the ball to create anti-clockwise spin.

Do this for some time and don't rush it until, very gradually, you start to see the ball moving from right to left. When that happens, you can start increasing the length of your swing, working slowly up from halfswings to a full swing.

PRO TIP

In order to promote the idea of hitting a draw when you are teeing off, tee the ball really high. That will automatically force you to sweep through the ball and encourage a feeling of hitting around it.

LEFT When playing a draw from the tee, position the ball on the far left of the tee box. You can then swing to the right which will encourage the draw shot.

ABOVE Practising hitting shots with your right hand only is a great way to learn and understand the draw. Imagine you are playing a topspin table tennis shot as you make your swing and watch the ball move right to left.

THE FADE SHOT

Most players already naturally hit a fade, or its ugly sibling, the slice. Lee Trevino, the master of hitting the ball left to right, once said that you can talk to a fade but you can't talk to a hook.

Like a slice, a hook will make the ball run into all sorts of trouble. But when you hit the ball with a soft fade, at least you know the ball is going to stop nicely.

That's the beauty of this shot. The fade is ideal when you are faced with a left-to-right dogleg from the tee, when you have to bend the ball the same way around a hazard, or when you need to get more height to clear a tree and land the ball softly.

HOW TO PLAY THE FADE

ABOVE If you tee the ball on the right-hand side of the teeing ground, it will encourage you to aim left and hit the fade shot.

LEFT When you play the fade shot, aim slightly left of the target, move your grip fractionally to the left (a weaker grip), play the ball slightly further forward in your stance and picture the ball moving left to right.

High shot

Unlike the draw, the fade is a high shot that will not run very much when the ball reaches the ground. That makes it a great shot for long approaches to the green, but much trickier to use in the wind.

That's the good news.

The bad news is that the average golfer will not get as much distance with a fade.

Since most golfers tend to lack penetration with their shots anyway, always playing a fade is going to put you at an immediate disadvantage. In fact, most golfers would be better off trying to generate a draw in their swing, and using that particular option as their normal shot.

Having said that, knowing how to fade the ball is necessary for a variety of situations and it's an essential weapon in your golfing armoury if you truly want to improve your game.

ABOVE To encourage the fade you can play the ball slightly further forwards – but don't overdo it!

How to hit a fade

To hit a fade, open your stance by moving your front foot back off the target line. Aiming left, align your feet, hips and shoulders in an open stance that points to 11 o'clock on the imaginary clockface. In terms of swingpath, think about moving out-to-in, pulling the club across the ball from 5 to 11. That will impart clockwise spin.

Adjusted grip

The next thing you should do is to adjust your grip. If you naturally draw the ball, you will have to turn your hands round to the left – or 'weaken' your grip. This may be an advantage for some, but if you already hit the ball from left to right – or with a fade – it's important not to overdo this adjustment. Opening your hands – or moving them more to the left – could produce a massive slice.

Remember that every change we make to create a golf shot has to be relative to your game. So for the natural slicer, simply opening the stance a bit and aiming slightly left might be enough to produce the correct swingpath.

Ball position

Let's assume you hit the ball straight and go from there. To hit a fade, especially if you want more height, you need to play the ball slightly more forward in your stance than usual – about an inch (2.5cm) further forward should be enough. In simple terms, that means playing it off your left heel.

However, if you already play the ball from inside your left heel, you do not need to move it further forward for a fade. Playing any shot with the ball too far up in your stance will cause you to pull it – or hit straight left.

Weaken the grip by turning the hands fractionally to the left.

PRO TIP

Remember that a fade will cost you distance, especially if you try to add more height to the shot. So take that into consideration when visualizing what you are about to do and selecting your club. In addition, if you are fading into the wind, you will lose considerable length, so go up two or more clubs if possible to compensate for that.

KEYS TO THE FADE SWING

I like to play a fade a little bit more from my left side. After taking an open set-up, I swing back along the line of my stance, without modifying anything in my backswing. Since I am aiming left, I have already swung naturally outside the target line.

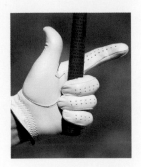

To encourage the fade, grip the club slightly firmer with the top three fingers of the left hand. Keep the right hand relaxed.

But when I come through the ball, I want to cut across the same line and move the club inside by delaying the release of the clubhead just a fraction.

Relaxed hand

How do I accomplish that? The first thing I do is relax my right hand at address, and then grip the club a little bit tighter with the last three fingers of my left hand – the little, ring and middle fingers. In other words, the right hand stays very light, while the leading hand grips just a bit firmer.

When I come through the ball, I then try to feel as though I'm delaying the release of the clubhead just a bit, or simply preventing the club from coming through as early as normal. That should be enough to hit slightly across the ball.

However, this does not mean that I do not release the clubhead! What it means is the release comes just slightly later than it would for a regular shot. Apart from that, I just swing normally.

Avoiding trouble

Professional golfers routinely move the ball in various directions in order to avoid trouble on one side of a golf course or the other. If the trouble is on the right, they'll hit a draw. If it's on the left, they'll play a fade. The key is actually to start the ball towards the trouble spot, then move it away.

The 18th hole on the championship West Course at Wentworth is a good example. This is a classic set-up for a fade because the hole doglegs left to right, with a big bunker on the left. Most pros will hit the

When you are trying to fade the ball off the tee with a wood, tee the ball down (above). This is especially useful when you're under pressure and there's trouble on the left. By teeing the ball down you are almost certain to fade the ball with a driver.

To play the fade shot, imagine you are swinging from 5 to 11 o'clock, moving the club across the ball on an out-to-in path. Feel more left-side control as you swing forwards with the left hand leading the clubhead through the ball.

ball at the bunker and then let it slide. So if you ever play Wentworth, I would suggest you tee the ball low on the 18th, get out your driver, and hit it straight at the bunker, gripping a little bit tighter with those last three fingers of the left hand.

You will pull the club through the ball as you do normally. But because you're hitting with the leading hand gripping just slightly tighter than the other hand, the clubface will come through a split second later. That will impart the necessary spin to curve the ball away from the bunker.

Use less loft

If you're hitting a wood and want almost to ensure you fade the ball, the less loft the better. In other words, if you normally hit a 3-wood off the tee, take a driver. And if you usually employ a 5-wood off the fairway, you might want to drop down to a 3.

The 3-wood is easier to fade because it makes the ball spin more than the loft on a 5-wood. In addition, you might even try hitting a driver off the fairway. To hit a draw in that situation is virtually impossible, but you have a chance if you try to fade the ball.

PRO TIP

If you are on the tee and want to make sure you don't hook the ball because there is real trouble down the left-hand side, tee the ball low and take out your driver. Now think about hitting a fade. With the ball so low to the ground, and the driver in your hand, it's almost impossible to hook. Instead, your natural instinct will produce a fade, because you'll be thinking you virtually have to swing from out to in on the ball to make it get airborne.

BE PROPERLY EQUIPPED TO CREATE BACKSPIN

The better the player you become, the more you will find yourself in situations where you want to apply backspin to the ball. For this, you must have a good technique and the right equipment.

ABOVE Different metals used in the manufacture of clubheads make a significant difference to how much backspin you can create.

You might want to land the ball on a green with a hard surface and a tough pin placement. You might be aiming at a green surrounded by bunkers and long rough – with no way to run the ball up to it. Or you might even be going over water to an island green and need to stop the ball within only a few feet of landing. In these situations, knowing how to apply backspin to the ball is essential.

Great precision

If you are going to start working on putting backspin on the ball, you must first be a competent player. That's because the only way to create backspin is by being able to strike the ball with great precision – if you strike the ball poorly, you'll never create any backspin. This is truly an advanced technique, only worth learning if your swing is reliable and solid.

The right ball

Having a great swing is the first, but not the only, requirement for applying backspin to the ball with a wedge or other short iron. In this case, both the type of ball you use and having the right equipment are major contributing factors.

Only one type of ball will allow you to create effective backspin – the balata. But most amateur golfers use a two-piece, surlyn-covered ball because it's cheaper, wears considerably longer, and goes further when struck well.

Balata-covered balls are expensive, cut easily and mean a sacrifice in distance. They allow you to apply backspin because the soft balata cover, in conjunction with the liquid centre and wound construction inside the ball, compresses more than conventional golf balls when struck precisely. As a result, the balata ball actually stays on the clubface longer, rotating up the blade and gathering anti-clockwise spin – which helps generate backspin and stops the ball on landing.

Mild steel and soft inserts

Another factor in creating backspin is the material used in your clubs. Your wedges should be made from softer metal than the hard steel used in a 2-iron. Many of the best wedges feature clubfaces of mild steel with chrome plating. Some also have a copper insert. These materials help the ball stay on the clubface longer and, once again, will create more backspin and help ball control.

FAR LEFT If you hit consistently, a balata ball gives you more control around the greens.

CENTRE AND LEFT A clean and dry clubface is essential to applying backspin. Try to make a habit of tidying up wedges after every strike with a tee or groove cleaner.

SWING KEYS TO APPLYING BACKSPIN

The key to applying backspin is to develop a very precise strike on the ball. You have to make sure you hit the ball before you hit anything else.

ABOVE Never try to lift the ball upwards – simply swing forward to your target.

If you hit the ground even slightly before you hit the ball, you will fail to create backspin. Focus on the top of the ball, to help you to make clean contact. I also play a more out-to-in type of swing, almost trying to fade the ball. That makes me think about hitting down and across the ball. Coming at the ball from out to in gives me a better chance of hitting crisply.

Take a divot

I also try to take a divot. With the shorter irons, I'm already hitting on a slightly downward path, and this helps to create backspin as it will make the ball spin up the clubface. But hitting down on the ball too much runs the risk of chopping the clubface into the ground – either before or after impact with the ball.

Both mistakes will affect the strike. Remember that you want to take a divot, but you do not want simply to hit down, so ensure that you hit down and forward towards your target. As with any golf shot, you always want to be going forwards and through the ball.

Because you are using a short, lofted club, you will be bent over more. Be careful not to exaggerate your action otherwise you'll end up taking a huge divot.

To apply increased backspin, you need to open your stance, with your weight slightly favouring your left side. Take the club away with your arms and break your wrists early to produce a sharp downward strike into the ball. Use a three-quarter swing, keep your hands ahead of the clubface, and keep your weight transfer down to a minimum.

Clean strike

The priority here is not distance but a clean strike. A more compact swing helps you to make a precise strike, because, with your weight favouring the left side and your hands ahead of the club, you will naturally hit the ball with a descending blow.

If, instead, you try to lift the ball with your club, your weight will probably stay on the back foot, which will cause you to hit the ground first with the clubhead or top the ball. Trying to scoop the ball upwards is a major fault of many golfers – you must strike down to hit the ball up, letting the loft of the clubface produce a high-flying shot.

LEFT To help create backspin I open my stance, keep my weight forward and break my wrists quite early in my backswing. This results in a sharp downward strike on the ball.

THE BUMP AND RUN

The bump and run is an effective shot when you are trying to keep the ball low under the wind, playing off hard ground, or simply trying to run the ball up to a green. The shot is much easier to judge and control than a high pitch, and is ideal when you do not have to fly bunkers, water or rough to reach the green.

These are two clubs you may consider when playing the bump and run shot.

Most golfers associate this shot with links courses, where the bump and run is often employed to avoid the tricky winds that characterize such courses. Playing target golf in these circumstances can be a disaster. When the ball gets airborne, it can be blown off line, especially with a wedge.

But the bump and run can be used on any course under the right conditions – or the wrong ones for that matter.

Thin hopes

In the summer, when the fairways tend to dry out, the bump and run is also useful because it allows for a wide margin of error. Even if you thin the ball, it will still run forwards along your intended line, perhaps accomplishing pretty much what you had hoped for in the first place.

BELOW Here I'm playing a shot from around 65 yards (60m) from the hole. My stance is fairly open, with hips and feet pointing left of target and the ball set back in my stance. I take a half to three-quarter swing.

Using the bump and run to an uphill green is also a great idea, since it's easy to misjudge the distance and park a lofted shot on the bank and short – or fly the green completely.

You can use a variety of clubs for the bump and run, and hit the shot anywhere from 60 to 160 yards (55 to 145m), making the bump and run one of golf's most versatile shots.

The approach shot

As with any golf shot, club selection is the first important decision you must make.

You can play a bump and run with anything from a sand wedge to a 6-iron, depending on what you want to do. It's a good idea to practise a variety of shots at the range using different clubs to get a feel for how each club plays in different situations.

Selecting the right club will have a lot to do with how far you want the ball to fly before it starts running, or what you want it to clear initially. If you are playing a links course and have a lot of humps and

BUMP AND RUN

ABOVE The length of the back- and throughswings should control the distance you will hit the ball.

Playing the ball along the ground with a putter from up to 50 yards (46m) can be very successful. Ensure that the ground is dry and that there are no obstacles (such as sprinkler heads) in between you and the hole. And remember, never up, never in!

bumps ahead which might deflect the ball off the target line, you may want to take many of them out by flying the ball further. That may demand a wedge. But if you really want to keep the ball flat to the ground, or low and running most of the way, then you might choose a 6-iron.

Control and feel

I'll use a 60-yard (55m) shot to the green as a typical example of when one might use a bump and run. In that case, you might want the ball to fly 40 yards (37m) and roll 20 yards (18m).

Take out the wedge and choke halfway down the grip for better control and feel.

Then open your stance, with the hips and feet pointing slightly left of the target, but the shoulders remaining parallel to the target line.

The shoulders should be positioned as they would be for a conventional shot because the last thing I want to do is to hit the ball with an out-to-in

swingpath. Ideally, I want the club actually to come from a slightly in-to-out direction, which will help get the ball running.

Going low

Now I set the ball back in my stance, from the centre to slightly behind that, which helps make the ball fly lower. In turn, my hands are set ahead of the clubhead, which helps deloft the club and also helps make the ball run low.

Finally, I set my weight towards the left side and keep it there. I don't want much weight transfer when making this shot.

BUMP AND RUN WITH A PUTTER
A shot that often can be very successful is a bump and run with a putter. I have used my putter from up to 50 yards (46m) from the green if there are no hazards, conditions are dry and the grass is short.

SWING KEYS TO THE BUMP AND RUN

Once I am set up properly for the bump and run, I plan to take a half to three-quarter swing, depending on the length of my approach, trying to keep even and balanced throughout.

RIGHT Remember to allow for contours in the ground as they will affect the run of your ball.

The most effective way to achieve that is to think about matching the length of the throughswing to that of the backswing. I also want to take the body out of this movement so I need to swing just with the arms and hands.

Smoothly done

A smooth, unhurried tempo is essential. It's very easy to rush these shots, especially with the sort of gusting winds that you get on seaside links – one moment you feel you are playing in a gale, then the wind drops, so you are then tempted to play the shot quickly in anticipation of the wind picking up.

The tendency is to get forwards too quickly. At the same time, you want to ensure you accelerate through the ball, with the feeling that you are almost squeezing it between the clubface and turf.

Remember, you want to create overspin on the ball to get it running, and from your set-up you will naturally be bringing the clubface from in-to-out – helping you to nip the ball off the ground.

When playing the bump and run, keep your hands well ahead of the clubhead as you make your throughswing.

Point skyward

Think of this shot as dominated by the left side. What you certainly do not want to do is to lift the ball by using too much right hand. So keep both hands ahead of the clubface, but lead the shot with the back of your left hand.

You don't want to break your wrists too much on the backswing, and you don't want to release the right arm on the throughswing. So visualize that, at the end of your swing, the back of your left hand will be facing up at the sky.

Letting the wrists break would lead to a chopping action on the ball, rather than promoting the idea of squeezing it off the turf to get a nice, flat trajectory.

The longer approach

You can use the bump and run for longer approaches to the green – from 100 yards (91m) out to even 160 yards (145m) – employing a sand wedge down to a 6-iron, although when you use the sand wedge you will need to deloft the face substantially. The approach on this shot is similar to when using a wedge from only 60 yards (55m).

Again, you want to take an open stance, but with the shoulders still parallel to the target line. Then use a three-quarter swing, with your weight and hands forward. Try to squeeze the ball off the turf by hitting down with a firm left wrist, making sure the swingpath is slightly in-to-out. Finish with your left wrist pointing at the sky.

Visualizing the shot

Once again visualization plays its part. This is especially important on a links-type course with a lot of humps and bumps.

If you were to hit a lofted club in this situation, and the ball came down on the wrong hump, it could fly off sideways or even worse. Running it in is a better option, because the ball can roll along with the contours of the land.

So pick a spot where you want the ball to land and try to imagine how the ball will react afterwards. Then focus on that spot – much as you would for a chip – and hit your shot.

Help for the weekend golfer

The bump and run is a great shot if you only play golf once a week. Trying to play target golf without hours of practice is difficult and frustrating. But if you hit more low runners than high-flying pitches during a round, you have the advantage of probably succeeding even if you mishit the ball.

With the bump and run, a semi-thinned shot will still produce a half-decent result – you are already anticipating running the ball.

When the ground is hard and dry, it's much safer and more predictable to keep the ball low. With the grass reasonably fine, the ball will trundle along nicely, reacting almost as it would on the green.

The bump and run requires you to make a low takeaway. Keep the weight principally on your left foot and then pull the club forwards with the hands staying well ahead of the clubhead through impact, as shown here.

THE LOB SHOT

The lob is one of the toughest shots in golf. But with the proper technique and lots of practice, many golfers can learn how to execute it consistently. You need this shot when you have to play over a hazard and then stop the ball quickly in a small landing area around the pin – sometimes as close as just a few feet away.

This shot requires the left hand to be in control through the ball.

Almost all professionals carry a lob wedge these days.

Only try the lob shot if you have grass beneath the ball. Don't even consider it if you're sitting on hard ground.

So the lob is a shot that you are sometimes *forced* to play, when you need to get over a hazard and stop the ball dead, rather than one you might occasionally choose in preference to other options.

I will play this shot from short range, from only 5 to 15 yards (4.5 to 13.5m) away – maybe 20 yards (18m) at the most. Trying to hit a lob shot from much further than that is getting into very dangerous territory – the sort of danger that beginners should not even contemplate!

Specialist club

The advent of the lob wedge has helped every golfer play this shot better. Of course, the pros can still open up their sand wedges and play the lob shot with great precision. But the average golfer risks thinning the ball

if he tries a similar technique. A sand wedge has a high degree of bounce, so opening the blade and trying to play this shot from low-cut grass, a tight lie or hardpan can be extremely problematic. However, if the lie is good and there is a lot of grass under the ball, a sand wedge might work for you.

Hitting the lob

When hitting the lob, the first thing you must do is open your stance, with your feet, hips and shoulders pointing left by 15 to 20 degrees. You must aim that far left to compensate for how far you are going to open the face of the sand wedge.

Now open up your wedge by as much as 8 degrees, depending on how high you want to lift the ball – really laying the clubface open.

Play the ball off the inside of your left heel or front foot, angling the club for an out-to-in swingpath with your weight favouring the left foot – aim for a ratio of about 60:40.

Really stable

You want real stability with this shot. Try to keep as centred as possible and keep your head still and your weight towards your left foot.

Take a three-quarter backswing with a sharp pick-up of the wrists. Then really try to feel the butt of the club coming through ahead of the clubhead, so that you pull across the ball.

I try to imagine almost slicing under the ball with the back of my left hand. That will help me shoot the ball quickly up in the air with lots of backspin, then let it drop down very softly.

More height

I can get even more height with a lob wedge because the club has so much more loft. I also don't need to open the face quite so much – if at all. The rest of the technique employed to hit the lob shot stays pretty much the same.

As with any shot, practise the lob regularly in order to build confidence – particularly as this is the sort of shot you bring out only in pressure situations.

THE LEFT SIDE IN CONTROL

The lob is one of the toughest shots in golf and requires lots of practice. Use the technique above to practise keeping the left side in control.

With the lob wedge I generally don't need to open the face like one does with a sand wedge as the club is very lofted anyway.

THE LOB FROM GREENSIDE ROUGH

Phil Mickelson excels at hitting soft lobs around the green, even from the sort of horrific rough typically found at the US Open. And although Mickelson takes a longer backswing than I recommend for most players – because he has the clubface so far open – emulating his method will help you escape from greenside rough.

Left-hander Phil Mickelson tries to get the ball as high as possible in order to compensate for the lack of backspin caused by the high grass. Even with a lob in this situation, you have to accept that the ball will run a bit on landing. But if you were to play a more conventional chip shot from such rough, the ball would run forever.

Less quit

Another reason to play a lob shot from greenside rough is because if you can really swing through it, you stand less chance of quitting on the ball. That's a big danger when playing out of this type of rough. The natural inclination is to let the club stay in the grass because your swing is inhibited.

If you hit the lob correctly, you will get some momentum on the clubhead as you come through, which produces the height as the loft on your wedge sends the ball up in the air.

Remember, it's easy for the clubface to snag on the long grass and close in the rough. But with the clubface so open initially – or naturally lofted in the case of the lob wedge – that will help prevent turning the club over.

BELOW Using a lob wedge from greenside rough allows you to accelerate through the shot, reducing the possibility of your club getting caught up in the long grass.

LOB SHOT FROM ROUGH

LOB FROM DOWNHILL ROUGH LIE

The only precaution when playing the lob wedge from the rough is that you have to take care not to pass clean under the ball without moving it forwards – most embarrassing!

PRO TIP

Even though you play a lob shot from greenside rough in a similar way to a bunker shot, be careful about hitting too far behind the ball. When I say you should play a splash shot, I am trying to emphasize technique, rather than the idea of hitting a few inches behind the ball. If the rough is deep enough, plenty of grass will inevitably come between the clubface and the ball, making contact slippery. Try to hit the ball as precisely as possible.

RIGHT TOP TO BOTTOM
A perfect use of the lob wedge.

PLAYING IN THE WIND

Great golfers learn how to use the wind to their advantage, and minimize the damage when that is not possible. So don't let the wind play on your mind, or you'll lose confidence – which leads to tension and ultimately a breakdown in your swing. Playing in the wind can be both challenging and fun, if you know what you are doing.

A tailwind can help you to increase your distance dramatically and actually help you to strengthen the fundamentals of your swing. On the other hand, hitting into the wind can reduce your distance, but aid you in stopping the ball quickly on the green and even impart some backspin.

Crosswinds are trickier. But once you learn how to hit into the windstream correctly and then let it carry your ball, you will be on the way to lowering your scores – even when the wind blows a gale.

BELOW The wind in your face is a real test of how much you believe in your golf swing.

BELOW RIGHT Looking at the tops of the trees will tell you more about the wind than conditions at ground level do. Use the knowledge to your advantage.

Using a tailwind

Most golfers automatically feel more comfortable with the wind at their backs because they know it will help them hit the ball further. However, unless they understand and employ certain advanced techniques for hitting in the wind, they'll never fully capitalize on that obvious advantage.

Decisions, decisions – choosing the right club is crucial in windy conditions.

FAR LEFT Wearing a hat can stop you hair blowing around – not that I have to worry too much about that!

LEFT A stable base to your golf swing is very important. If it's windy, I increase the width of my stance.

PRO TIP

Not enough players practise in the wind. If you are on the course on a windy day and it's quiet, drop some balls and experiment with a few clubs to see what effect the wind has on how each performs, and how the wind affects your natural ball flight.

Let's say you are on the tee of a long par 4 where you would normally play a driver. Every golfer knows that hitting a 3-wood off the tee generally guarantees more accuracy and control when it is struck properly, though distance is sacrificed. But in this situation hitting a 3-wood rather than the driver is the best play, because the added loft will get the ball up higher and into the prevailing wind.

In addition, even if you do not get a perfect strike on the ball, less sidespin will be imparted, and the ball will go straighter and further.

The same principle applies once you are on the fairway. Where you would normally use a 3-wood, you can now try the 5- or even 7-wood and get just as much distance – if not more because they are easier to hit – with the added benefit of more control.

Straighter flight

A tailwind will also straighten out your natural ball flight – whether you hit with a bit of fade or draw – because the wind reduces the amount of spin. That makes for a more penetrating hit and allows you to place the ball more accurately for your next shot.

Make sure you aim for the side of the fairway that will allow you to run the ball up to the green – using perhaps a long bump and run shot. Remember that you will never stop the ball on the putting surface with a high wedge shot in a tailwind.

You should also know that the ball will kick and run on from your tee shot, so mentally you need to allow for that. As for approach shots, a strong tailwind will produce enough boost to move a 7- or even 8-iron shot anything up to 200 yards (183m). Golfers often cannot convince themselves of that fact. They may take the correct club, but when they get to the top of their backswing, they suddenly panic and think they have not got enough club. They then end up forcing the shot and overshoot.

Assess the effect of the wind, select a club and then keep faith with the shot you have decided to hit.

BELOW Keep the swing compact and this will help you to maintain control while others around you are flailing away.

PLAYING INTO A HEADWIND

Hitting into a headwind will increase the spin on the ball, which is an excellent incentive for firing confidently at the pin, and trusting the ball to stop quickly on the green. But if you are on the tee or facing a long shot from the fairway, you have to remember that this aspect of hitting into the wind will exaggerate any problems you have with the long woods and irons.

BELOW Tee the ball high and aim to sweep the ball clean off the tee.

If you hit a driver with a bit of draw, playing with the wind in your face could change that shot into a hook. Alternatively, if you hit the ball with a nice little fade, that could become an ugly slice. You have to make allowances for these tendencies, or you will pay a significant price.

Play it safe and smooth

Take the safest route up the fairway that you can, choosing one side or the other while accepting the fact that you will lose considerable distance – perhaps as much as 50 to 75 yards (46 to 69m) on a drive. But this is better than parking the ball in the rough or something worse.

BELOW A combination of stability and compactness are the keys to playing in the wind.

Try teeing the ball higher than normal, then think about picking it clean off the top in an attempt to hit a penetrating shot that flies low into the wind.

Tempo is also a key here. You have to maintain your composure and keep a smooth, even rhythm to your swing. Losing it in the wind can destroy your game very, very quickly.

Three-club wind

Once you are down on the fairway, play very conservatively and remember that you might have to hit one, two or three more clubs than you usually would to achieve certain distances. How often have you heard people say that a 30mph (50km/h) wind is 'a three-club wind'? If you've ever played in such winds, you know the truth of that phrase all too well.

Hitting a golf ball into a headwind is one situation where playing the long irons, rather than utility woods, is a good idea. Using a 5- or 7-wood in strong

GOOD BALANCE IN WINDY CONDITIONS

wind
direction

winds is not advisable because the ball will just shoot into the air. But the 3- and 4-irons can really play their parts superbly in these situations, because they will help you keep the ball flat.

Even a driver off the fairway is worth trying, if you have practised the shot on the range. In an emergency, with the wind against you, hit a little three-quarter swing with the big club, trying to keep your movement as smooth as possible.

Don't worry about mishitting the ball, because you might get a better result than using something like a 5-wood, since the ball will stay flat. But even if you top it, that's better than hitting the ball up in the air, where it can go just about anywhere.

Staying safe

Whatever club you use on the fairway, be certain to look for the safest route to approach the green – and don't try anything too ambitious. So if the hole is a par 4, expect it to take you three shots, or perhaps even four, just to reach the green.

Think to yourself that if you two-putt from there, it's a six, rather than the eight or nine you're more likely to record if you fly out of bounds or into significant trouble.

You can then take comfort from the fact that you are going to have a hole somewhere else on the golf course where the wind is with you. So you will have a chance to repair the damage to your score.

LEFT It's tough – but always visualize a positive outcome to your shot, even when the wind is howling around your ears and burning your face.

DRIVER OFF THE DECK

I would never recommend hitting a driver off the fairway in normal circumstances – especially for the beginner or high-handicap player who should also avoid using a 3-wood anywhere except from the tee. But if you are an experienced golfer, possess a solid, repeatable swing, and have the confidence to attempt this shot, I recommend it for playing in the wind. The first thing to consider is the lie. Hitting a driver off the fairway demands an excellent lie, so always avoid a tight lie or any situation where the ball is sitting even slightly down. Put the ball about an inch (2.5cm) further back in your stance than you would off the tee and try to keep your hands slightly ahead of the ball at impact. If you make solid contact, the ball should take off with a low, penetrating line of flight.

COURSES

Golf is one of the few sports where the average player can play on the same stage as the stars and encounter the same problems – even at the spiritial home of golf, St Andrews.

ST ANDREWS
THE OLD COURSE, ST ANDREWS, FIFE, SCOTLAND

'How do you grow grass like that?' enquired an American golfing visitor to St Andrews, the charming, ancient university town known worldwide as the 'Home of Golf.'

'Sow the seed and let it grow for 500 years,' replied his local caddie.

RIGHT The dreaded bunker which guards the 17th, the Road Hole, perhaps the most feared par-4 in golf. Beyond, the 18th provides a grandstand finish to the world's most famous course in front of the R&A clubhouse.

Golf's spiritual home

It is not known exactly when golf started to be played here – the first written mention of it is 1552 – but since 1754, when the Royal and Ancient Golf Club of St Andrews (R&A) was founded, its influence on the development of golf worldwide has been immense. However, the R&A does not own the golf courses, which are run by the Links Management Trust on behalf of the town. Residents are entitled to annual permits giving them various playing rights over the public courses for a modest sum. Visitors from further afield may book online, by post or by telephone far in advance, take advantage of one of the golf tour operators' packages, or take pot luck in the daily ballot.

BOBBY JONES

The Old Course has not appealed to everyone on first sight. Bobby Jones tore up his card on first playing there, but he later came to appreciate its merits saying, 'I could take out of my life everything except my experiences at St Andrews and I'd still have a rich, full life.'

The ultimate opening drive

Standing on the 1st tee the golfer is presented with the widest fairway imaginable, downhill, shared with the 18th and not a single bunker to trap the wayward shot. Strong players could drive the green were it not for the Swilcan Burn which crosses in front. Yet that opening drive is nerve-racking for many, for it is played in front of the big windows of the R&A clubhouse and even at the crack of dawn there is usually a crowd of golfers and locals gathered on the terrace just watching the golf. A four here is always welcome.

Shared fairways and double greens

From the 2nd tee everything changes. The course stretches away in front, its fairways tumbling over crumpled ground, giving all manner of different lies and stances. Bunkers litter the place, very often in the most unexpected places, and the first-time visitor is wise to employ a caddie, for it is far from obvious what the best line might be on any given hole.

Much depends on where the hole has been cut on the giant double greens which characterize the Old Course. Such are the subtleties of the approaches to the greens that a given pin position might be impossible from all but a specific spot on the fairway.

In the last round of the 2005 Open Championship Tiger Woods had the luxury of watching his pursuers trying to attack the pins in order to pick up shots. More often than not they simply could not get their approaches close to the hole, quite often ending up three-putting, while Woods could play safely to the middle of the green and two-putt for par. He won the 2000 Open by playing such thoughtful golf that he never went in a single bunker in 72 holes of play!

Sting in the tail

Every hole has a name, every bunker, too, and there is a tale to be told of one famous golfer or another coming to grief at some time. The catalogue of disasters on the 17th hole is legendary, the entire play of the hole dominated by one very nasty bunker eating into the heart of the green and the road which passes on the other side of this inaccessible, table-top green. And if the 18th, like the 1st, is bunkerless, nobody is safe from calamity until the Valley of Sin has been negotiated at the front of the green.

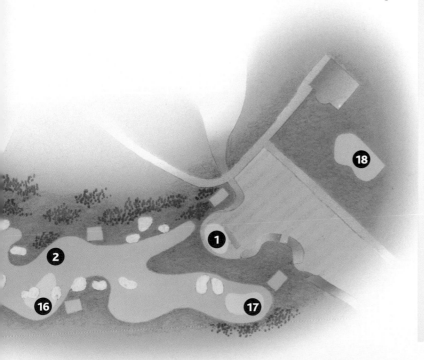

	Hole	Distance (yards)	Par
1	Burn	376	4
2	Dyke	453	4
3	Cartgate (out)	397	4
4	Ginger Beer	480	4
5	Hole o' Cross (out)	568	5
6	Heathery (out)	412	4
7	High (out)	390	4
8	Short	175	3
9	End	352	4
10	Bobby Jones	380	4
11	High (in)	174	3
12	Heathery (in)	348	4
13	Hole o' Cross (in)	465	4
14	Long	618	5
15	Cartgate (in)	456	4
16	Corner of the Dyke	423	4
17	Road	455	4
18	Tom Morris	357	4
	Out	3,603	36
	In	3,676	36
	Total	7,279	72

CARD OF THE COURSE

ROYAL ST GEORGE'S
ROYAL ST GEORGE'S GOLF CLUB, SANDWICH, KENT, ENGLAND

The first 33 Open Championships were played in Scotland, at Prestwick, Musselburgh, St Andrews and Muirfield. In 1894 it moved south for the first time, to Sandwich on the Kent coast of England. The club was founded by a pair of Scottish golfers, Dr Laidlaw Purves and Henry Lamb, who, in the 1880s, were touring the south coast, desperately searching for a patch of land on which to build a golf course along the lines of the great Scottish links. They spied what they were looking for, some of the most dramatic linksland in the whole of Britain, from the church tower in Sandwich.

Traditional links features

Most probably Purves himself designed the first course here, which opened in 1887. It was about 6,000 yards (5,500m) long, viciously bunkered, narrow and full of blind shots. J.H. Taylor's winning score in the 1894 Open Championship was 326, the highest total ever. Harry Vardon won the next Open played at Sandwich with a total of 310, and when the Open returned in 1904 Vardon recorded a round of 69, the first time 70 had been beaten.

These days the worst of the blind shots have been eliminated, but the ground still has plenty of movement and many competitors in the 2003 Open Championship found that they could not hold the final fairway with their drives, so great was the sideways movement imparted on the ball by the ground. On the other hand, so powerful are today's top players that many attempted to drive the 5th green, 421 yards (385m) distant!

Awesome bunkers

From a tee beside a thatched starter's hut an inviting opening drive is made, the course heading for the sea. It is a tricky opening hole, for a depression, the Kitchen, crosses the fairway at about the length of a fair drive, with bunkers fronting the green awaiting an approach shot which is not quite good enough. The eye is deceived by a ridge on the 2nd, and the 3rd is a sturdy short hole created in 1975 by Frank Pennink.

One of the most forbidding bunkers in golf confronts the player on the 4th tee, a tall, sleepered affair set into a vast mound straight in front. There is no alternative, it simply has to be cleared and there is another, lesser bunker on the left beyond it to prevent anyone sneaking round the side.

From here on the golf is glorious, switching back and forth through and over the dunes so that the wind must be tackled from every quarter and with lovely views over Pegwell Bay from the higher ground. The fine 13th takes play to the farthest corner of the course, adjacent to Prince's Golf Club where the 1932 Open was staged.

From there the dangerous 14th is played hard alongside the boundary fence, beyond which is out of bounds. A stream, known as the Suez Canal, crosses the fairway at the length of a good drive, and the out of bounds and bunkers continue to threaten on the approach. It has wrecked the chances of many Open aspirants. Three strong par 4s and a testing short hole keep the challenge up to the very end.

ABOVE RIGHT A packed gallery watches Tiger Woods putting on the 6th – the most famous of Royal St George's short holes – during the final round of the 2003 Open Championship.

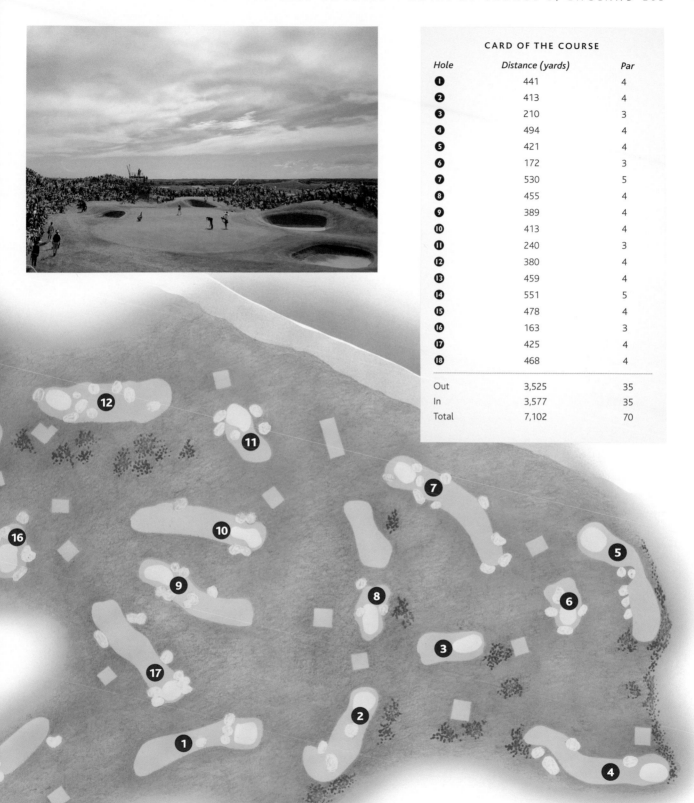

CARD OF THE COURSE

Hole	Distance (yards)	Par
1	441	4
2	413	4
3	210	3
4	494	4
5	421	4
6	172	3
7	530	5
8	455	4
9	389	4
10	413	4
11	240	3
12	380	4
13	459	4
14	551	5
15	478	4
16	163	3
17	425	4
18	468	4
Out	3,525	35
In	3,577	35
Total	7,102	70

WENTWORTH
WEST COURSE, THE WENTWORTH CLUB, VIRGINIA WATER, SURREY, ENGLAND

To the left of the A30 as you head southwest out of Virginia Water is the vast estate of Wentworth. Within it can be found the opulent houses of top sportsmen, venture capitalists and a film star or two. Three golf courses roam the estate which is centred on the 18th-century gothic-style country house originally built for the brother-in-law of the future Duke of Wellington. The estate was developed by George Tarrant, who had previously built the prestigious St George's Hill estate. There he had called in Harry Colt to design two courses. Colt was, therefore, the obvious choice to build two courses at Wentworth.

The East was the first to open, which it did in 1924, and it staged a match in 1926 between teams of professional golfers from Britain and America, which developed into the Ryder Cup. In that year the West Course opened, too. The Edinburgh Course is a much later addition, opening in 1990. It was designed by John Jacobs with the assistance of Gary Player and Bernard Gallacher.

The 'Burma Road'

Television has brought considerable prominence to the West Course as it hosts the annual PGA Championship in May and the World Matchplay (dating back to 1964) in the autumn, two of the most important events in the European calendar. Although the length of the West and its difficulty led to its nickname 'Burma Road', at around 7,000 yards (6,400m) from the professional tees it is not excessive by the standards of today.

In fact, winning scores in the PGA are usually in the low 270s. However, it is a very good matchplay venue for the mischief of some of the shorter two-shot holes becomes apparent. It can be very dangerous having to attack pins when holes are slipping away and many have come to grief on seemingly innocuous holes such as the 16th.

Searching test of golf

Members play the 1st hole as a par 5, but for the professionals it is a par 4, their huge drives often running down the slope of the valley on the far side of which sits the green, an awkward target from distance. The 2nd is also played across a valley, a very good example of a short hole which is still tricky despite its lack of length. It is followed by a tough uphill hole with a three-level green on which no one wants to have to putt downhill. From here the course winds through the estate until the long par-4 9th – demanding even for professionals – is played alongside the railway.

The 10th is an excellent short hole, its green narrow and angled. Trees block out the green on the 11th and 13th holes if the drive is made too far to the left and between them the 12th is a good birdie opportunity for the better player – both height and distance are required on the drive in order to clear trees in front and open up the green. It is difficult to judge the shot on the uphill 14th, the green being on two levels and sloping, and the 15th green has more borrow than at first sight it seems.

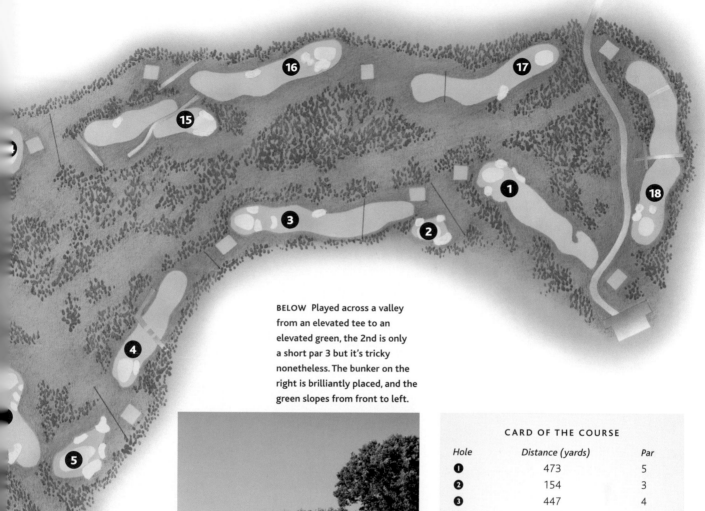

BELOW Played across a valley from an elevated tee to an elevated green, the 2nd is only a short par 3 but it's tricky nonetheless. The bunker on the right is brilliantly placed, and the green slopes from front to left.

Arnold Palmer reckoned the 17th to be one of the great par-5 holes – it is treacherous with out of bounds and overhanging trees on the left and the fairway leaning to the right as it curves left round the trees. Another par 5 closes the round, providing another opportunity to the professional for a birdie or even an eagle.

CARD OF THE COURSE

Hole	Distance (yards)	Par
1	473	5
2	154	3
3	447	4
4	497	5
5	191	3
6	354	4
7	396	4
8	400	4
9	452	4
10	184	3
11	403	4
12	509	5
13	442	4
14	179	3
15	481	4
16	383	4
17	571	5
18	531	5
Out	3,364	36
In	3,683	37
Total	7,047	73

PINE VALLEY
PINE VALLEY GOLF CLUB, CLEMENTON, NEW JERSEY, USA

In any discussion of the most penal courses in golf the name of Pine Valley will be raised. It was described by *The World Atlas of Golf* as 'George Crump's 184-acre bunker' but that is just one of the perils. Quite simply, at Pine Valley if you are not on the fairway or green you don't stand a chance.

Crump was a Philadelphia hotel owner who was prepared to pour $250,000 of his own money into a project he started in 1912. Sadly, he died in 1918 with only 14 holes completed. Crump had made the original routing and with later design input from Hugh Wilson, the English architect Harry Colt, and possibly Colt's partner Hugh Alison, the course was completed in time for opening in 1919.

Pine Valley does not feature in the lists of great championship courses. The plain fact is that it could not because there is nowhere for spectators to stand. You are either in sand or in the trees. It has hosted a couple of Walker Cup matches, but that is about all. But let no one doubt its quality.

Islands in the sand

The first four holes form a loop returning to the clubhouse. They are superb holes with the delicate pitch to the 2nd green and all-or-nothing shot to the 3rd hole among the highlights. But then comes the 5th, one of the most savage short holes in existence, a huge carry over water and scrub to a far-distant elevated green. This is not for the faint-hearted!

The 6th offers little respite before the extraordinary 7th is encountered. On this heroic par 5 there are two islands of fairway and a green. Unfortunately they are separated by a minor desert and unless each shot is hit with the utmost precision both for line and length there is no hope of salvation.

CARD OF THE COURSE

Hole	Distance (yards)	Par
1	427	4
2	367	4
3	181	3
4	444	4
5	232	3
6	388	4
7	567	5
8	319	4
9	427	4
10	146	3
11	392	4
12	344	4
13	448	4
14	184	3
15	591	5
16	433	4
17	338	4
18	428	4
Out	3,352	35
In	3,304	35
Total	6,656	70

ABOVE Each of the short holes at Pine Valley is notably uncompromising. This is the all-or-nothing 10th, with its particularly punishing pot bunker at the front.

Relentless back nine

A similar hole follows the same direction along the perimeter of the course on the back nine, the 13th. Again the hole is a succession of islands, this time two of them as the hole is a par 4. The problem is not so much finding the first stretch of fairway but more of getting the second shot to the angled green without falling foul of the sandy waste (nominally a bunker) lining the left side of the fairway and angled green. It is part of a terrifying run of holes, the 14th being played to an island green surrounded by water, the 15th another monstrous par 5 on which nothing other than the straightest of shots will suffice.

The trouble with Pine Valley is that this pressure is kept up for 18 holes.

ARNOLD PALMER

The story is told that the members of Pine Valley used to bet that no visitor playing the course for the first time could break 80. The young Arnold Palmer came to Pine Valley in 1954, then the reigning US Amateur Champion. He risked all, took on the members' bets and scored a 68. He came away with enough money to get married.

AUGUSTA
AUGUSTA NATIONAL GOLF CLUB, AUGUSTA, GEORGIA, USA

The first so-called Major of the golfing year, the Masters, is unique in that it is always played on the same course, Augusta National. At Masters time – April – the course is ablaze with colour, for it was laid out on the former nursery of the Belgian baron, Louis Mathieu Edouard Berkmans, the noted horticulturist who popularized the azalea in the United States. Augusta National was the brainchild of Bobby Jones, the astonishingly gifted amateur golfer who won four US Opens, three Open Championships, five US Amateurs and one British Amateur, including all four championships in one year, 1930. He then retired from competitive golf – at the age of only 28!

Strategic design

Having found the ideal site for his dream golf course, Jones enlisted the services of Alister MacKenzie, a Yorkshire-born Scotsman who had recently emigrated to America and was in great demand as a golf course architect. He settled in California where two of his outstanding designs, Pasatiempo and Cypress Point, were brought to Jones's attention.

Jones immediately recognized MacKenzie's flair for strategic, rather than penal, design. Jones had it in mind that Augusta would be a course that his high-handicap friends could get round without too much punishment, yet it should tax the top players whom he would invite every year for a tournament.

As designed, Augusta, then, had wide fairways with few bunkers and little or no rough. The key to its difficulty lay with its greens which were contoured and angled in such a way that only an approach shot played from one ideal spot on the fairway stood any chance of hitting and holding the green.

ABOVE The 18th hole provides a classic finish to the Masters, with a drive threatened by trees and bunkers on the elbow of the dogleg, and a second shot uphill to a tiered green.

Today's course

The course we see today is significantly different from that of the 1930s. The two nines have been reversed, a completely new 16th hole was added during Jones's lifetime and there have been alterations to the bunkering. However, the biggest change has been in the way the course is set up for the Masters. New tees have been built to stretch the course, fairways have been narrowed, trees planted and the greens are prepared at such frightening speeds that putting is almost, but not quite, impossible.

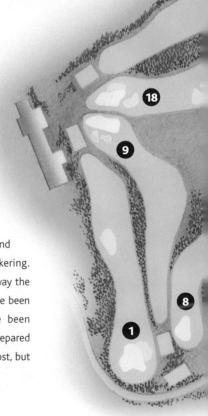

Amen Corner

The most treacherous part of the course is Amen Corner. The downhill 11th involves a drive that must be perfectly placed, for the approach shot is played to a slippery green guarded by a pond. While the 12th is only 155 yards (142m) long, the wind swirls in the valley making club selection difficult, the green broad but shallow and threatened by Rae's Creek and lurking bunkers. Rae's Creek comes into play on the 13th, a sharp dogleg with a gambling second shot played to a vast, rolling green encircled by the creek and bunkers.

BELOW Fickle winds, a narrow green, lurking bunkers and Rae's Creek make the par-3 12th a potential card-wrecker.

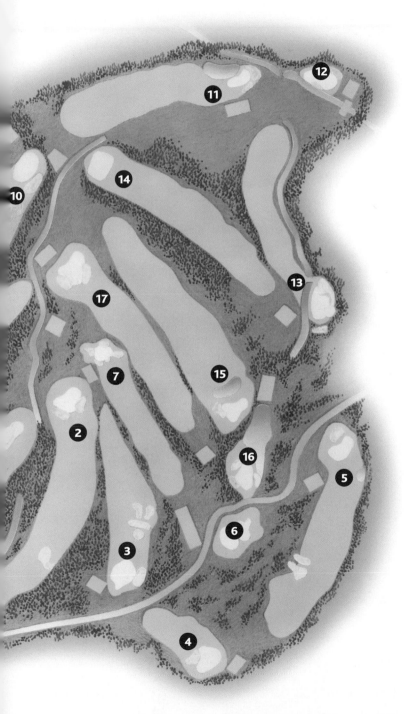

CARD OF THE COURSE		
Hole	*Distance (yards)*	*Par*
❶ Tea Olive	435	4
❷ Pink Dogwood	575	5
❸ Flowering Peach	350	4
❹ Flowering Crab Apple	205	3
❺ Magnolia	435	4
❻ Juniper	180	3
❼ Pampas	410	4
❽ Yellow Jasmine	570	5
❾ Carolina Cherry	460	4
❿ Camellia	495	4
⓫ White Dogwood	490	4
⓬ Golden Bell	155	3
⓭ Azalea	510	5
⓮ Chinese Fir	440	4
⓯ Firethorn	500	5
⓰ Redbud	170	3
⓱ Nandina	425	4
⓲ Holly	465	4
Out	3,620	36
In	3,650	36
Total	7,270	72

PEBBLE BEACH
PEBBLE BEACH GOLF LINKS, CALIFORNIA, USA

Host to the 1972, 1982, 1992 and 2000 US Open Championships, the 1929, 1947, 1961 and 1999 US Amateur Championships, umpteen AT&T Pebble Beach National Pro-Ams plus a host of Crosby Clambakes before that, Pebble Beach is a championship course par excellence. Unusually for the United States it is a public course. Anyone can play it – as long as they have deep pockets, and plenty of time in which to play their golf, for a round at Pebble Beach is not for the impatient.

Monterey Peninsula

There had been a luxury hotel, the Del Monte, near Monterey since 1880 and shortly after that 17 Mile Drive was opened, giving the public access to one of the most beautiful coastlines in the world. A 9-hole golf course opened in 1897, and in 1917 Samuel Morse was hired by the then landowners to develop the area for them. He, in turn hired Jack Neville, Douglas Grant and H. Chandler Egan to lay out a golf course worthy of such a site and the Pebble Beach Golf Links opened for play in 1919.

In those days this was quite a remote part of California, air travel was relatively primitive and the area became a quiet retreat for the wealthy of San Francisco and Los Angeles. Holding the 1929 US Amateur at Pebble was quite a bold step for the USGA to take at that time, but the event was a success and it brought Bobby Jones to this part of California (although he was knocked out quite early in the competition) which in turn led to his appointing Alister MacKenzie to help him build Augusta National. (Incidentally, MacKenzie made alterations to the 8th and 13th greens at Pebble in 1926.)

Glorious coast holes

Today Pebble Beach is part of an extraordinary complex of top-level golf courses, hotels, lodges and restaurants. It is certainly not remote any longer and bookings are taken years in advance. Although the course has been lengthened a little, not much has changed since it was first opened. For many years the

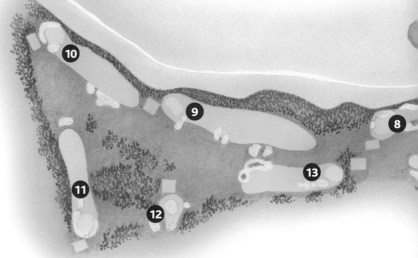

ABOVE One of golf's most photographed holes, the short 7th at Pebble Beach. Depending on the severity of the wind off the Pacific, anything from a wedge to a 3-iron is needed to reach the target.

course moved inland at the 5th hole, a short hole through the trees. However, in 1998 a new 5th hole alongside the sea was opened, to a design by Jack Nicklaus who had won both the US Amateur and US Open on this course. So now the course hits the shoreline on the short par-4 4th and hugs it all the way to the 10th green, one of the most exciting stretches of seaside golf imaginable.

The sequence of two-shot holes from the 8th to the 10th is both very demanding and also scenically distracting. However, it is the diminutive 7th hole, a par 3 of only 106 yards (97m) to a tiny green standing on the rocks at the water's edge, that is one of the most photographed holes in golf, and an absolute siren to play.

Watson's magic

If there is a tinge of regret at moving inland at the 11th it only serves to make the break out onto the shore at the 17th the more memorable, for this is a demanding short hole on which Tom Watson played one of the US Open's great shots in snatching the 1982 championship from Nicklaus. And Pebble keeps one of its finest holes for last, the gorgeous par 5 on which the merest pull finds the ball amongst the clams and oysters on the rocks.

CARD OF THE COURSE		
Hole	Distance (yards)	Par
1	376	4
2	502	5
3	374	4
4	327	4
5	187	3
6	500	5
7	106	3
8	416	4
9	462	4
10	430	4
11	373	4
12	210	3
13	393	4
14	572	5
15	396	4
16	401	4
17	178	3
18	543	5
Out	3,250	36
In	3,496	36
Total	6,746	72

BALLYBUNION
THE OLD COURSE, BALLYBUNION, COUNTY KERRY, EIRE

Ballybunion is now on the 'must play' list of anyone visiting Ireland to play golf. It was largely Tom Watson who popularized it when he visited it during his preparations for the 1975 Open Championship at Carnoustie, which he won. Watson had the vision and imagination to play all the improvized shots so necessary for successful links golf. He also had the temperament and the talent.

The Old Course at Ballybunion probably requires as much improvization as any links course in the British Isles. There is a historic reason for this. When the present course was first laid out in 1926 (although golf had been played here since the late 19th century) there was not the money in this remote part of Ireland to enter into lavish earth moving. The course was therefore set down on the land as they found it, resulting in a course which wanders over the dunes, along them and between them. Therefore many greens are set up on higher ground, requiring good judgement and a deft touch on the approach shot.

Finest piece of linksland

The American golf course designer Robert Trent Jones was given an unrivalled opportunity when in the 1980s he was invited to build a second course for the club. 'When I first saw the piece of land chosen for the new course of Ballybunion, I was thrilled beyond words. I said that it was the finest piece of linksland that I had ever seen, and perhaps the finest piece of linksland in the world.' The new course, known as the Cashen Course, is spectacular but also very difficult. The Old Course is gentler and yet every bit as good at examining every department of the golfer's game.

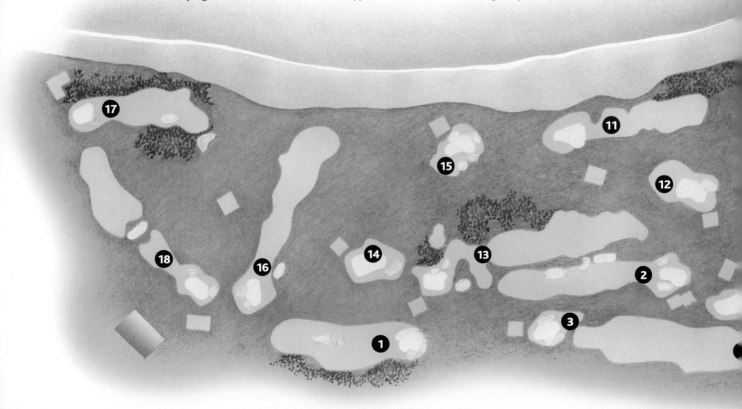

Atlantic backdrop

Perhaps more so at Ballybunion than at most other courses the measured length of the holes is less relevant, simply because of the topography and the varying strengths of the wind buffeting the course after its long journey across the Atlantic. In fact the start is earnest with two solid par 4s, a long par 3 and a couple of par 5s threatened by out of bounds. But the course has not really got under way until the approach is made to the 6th green, perched on top of the dunes and overlooking the ocean.

The 7th is a wonderful high-ground hole parallel to the ocean, and the 8th plunges inland, a hole described by Watson as having one of the most demanding tee shots he has faced. So nasty are the bunkers, humps and hollows surrounding the green that recovery can be a desperate business.

The hole that everyone anticipates most eagerly is the 11th, one of the greatest bunkerless holes in golf, but Ballybunion has not yet played all its trumps, for the 15th is a great short hole played over rough ground to a green backed by the ocean. Following that, the 16th is a delightful par 5 climbing back inland between the dunes before the 17th returns to the beach. If the final hole is a little more prosaic then there is less about it to delay the golfer from a refreshing pint of the dark stuff.

BELOW The 10th green and, beyond, the bunkerless 11th stretching back along the coast in among the dunes – links golf at its very best.

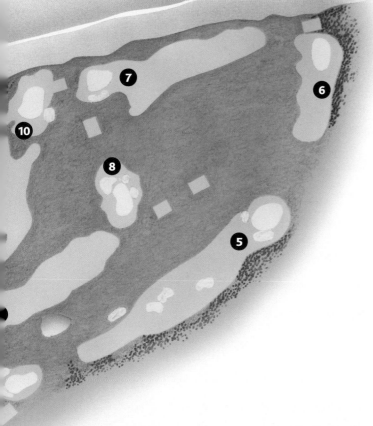

CARD OF THE COURSE

Hole	Distance (yards)	Par
1	400	4
2	439	4
3	220	3
4	529	5
5	552	5
6	382	4
7	420	4
8	153	3
9	456	4
10	361	4
11	451	4
12	200	3
13	486	5
14	135	3
15	212	3
16	499	5
17	376	4
18	379	4
Out	3,552	36
In	3,099	35
Total	6,651	71

VALDERRAMA
CLUB DE GOLF VALDERRAMA, SAN ROQUE, CADIZ, SPAIN

Valderrama began life as the New Course at Sotogrande, in turn becoming Las Aves, before being bought by Jaime Ortiz-Patiño, a Bolivian tin magnate who had retired to the area. Robert Trent Jones had designed the original course and Patiño decided to call him back to make a few alterations to fit it for the high quality tournament golf he wanted the course to host, featuring the world's top players. Most crucially, they reversed the two nines to provide a stronger finish, a massive drainage programme was initiated and, later, a lake was introduced in front of the 17th green. Since then it has played host to a number of Volvo Masters Andalucía tournaments, the traditional closing event of the European Tour, and the 1997 Ryder Cup.

ABOVE Outright length was never a priority at Valderrama and there are a number of short, but tricky, two-shot holes, such as the 14th.

The controversial 17th

The course has not been without criticism, but Patiño has listened to the critics and done something about it. For instance, controversy has surrounded the 17th green and an incident in 1999 when Tiger Woods' ball spun back from beyond the pin to finish in the water. Patiño lowered the hump on the right-hand side of the green by 4 inches (10cm) – and raised the front of the green by an inch and a half (4cm) and resurfaced the green. Tree pruning is an ongoing battle in an effort to keep the fairways at their full playing width but such is the depth of Patiño's pocket that Valderrama is undoubtedly one of the best conditioned courses in Europe.

Valderrama's overall length is modest, but the site is hilly and the wind is an omnipresent factor, particularly on those holes played across valleys, such as the par-3 15th. Club selection is never easy and while the trees which proliferate on the course may offer shelter from the wind on the tee, the ball will be at the mercy of gusts at the height of its flight.

The golden rule

Trees line the 1st fairway and give an indication of the demands on straightness the course will make. On the 2nd a tree stands in the middle of the fairway. It is referred to as the tree of the golden rule. It was not part of Trent Jones's design and he wished to remove it but the original developer, James McMicken, refused. 'Why?' said Jones. 'It's the golden rule,' said McMicken. 'What's that?' asked Trent. 'Simple,' replied McMicken. 'I have the gold, I make the rules!'

None of the short holes is easy, and the 3rd is a good example. Huge quantities of earth were moved to improve the 4th, making the green visible from the tee. A waterfall adds to the beauty, but it is a strategic hazard as well. The course switches direction frequently and how the rest of the front nine plays is actually dependent on which wind is blowing, the Poniente or Levante.

Professionals will certainly look for birdies on the 10th and 11th but the difficult 12th calls for perfect judgement with its green sloping from front to back. Muy Dificil (very difficult) describes accurately the 16th, the 17th is an exciting hole when the best players go for the green in two, and the final hole is all about keeping out of the trees, ideally driving out over them with a risky all-or-nothing shot.

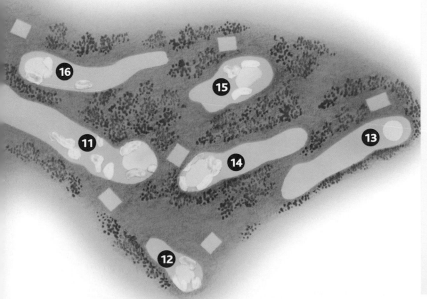

	Hole	Distance (m)	(yards)	Par
❶	Sol y Sombra	356	389	4
❷	El Arbol	385	421	4
❸	El Tunel	171	188	3
❹	La Cascada	516	565	5
❺	Los Altos	348	381	4
❻	El Vallejo	149	163	3
❼	El Mirador	487	533	4
❽	El Bunker	321	351	4
❾	El Muro	405	443	4
❿	El Lago	356	389	4
⓫	Un Sueño	500	547	5
⓬	Las Camelias	194	212	3
⓭	Sin Bunker	368	403	4
⓮	La Piedra	338	370	4
⓯	El Puerto	206	225	3
⓰	Muy Dificil	386	422	4
⓱	Los Gabiones	490	536	5
⓲	Casa Club	415	454	4
	Out	3,138	3,434	35
	In	3,253	3,558	36
	Total	6,391	6,992	71

CARD OF THE COURSE

ROYAL MELBOURNE
COMPOSITE COURSE, ROYAL MELBOURNE GOLF CLUB, BLACK ROCK, VICTORIA, AUSTRALIA

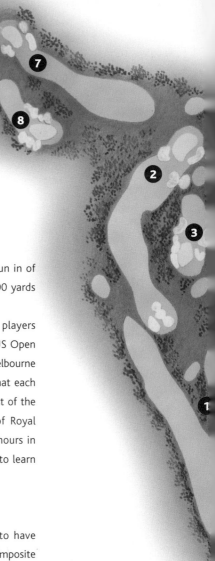

In England there is the Surrey heathland. In Australia there is the Melbourne sand belt. Some of the greatest inland courses in the world have been built here simply because of the nature of the soil and the grasses it supports. This was recognized early on, but Royal Melbourne's master stroke was to approach the R&A in 1926 seeking advice about who might best exploit their grounds with a view to making it a world class golf course. The R&A suggested Alister MacKenzie who visited Australia for two months which, according to the distinguished architect Tom Doak, changed a continent.

Royal Melbourne were clever in their negotiations with MacKenzie in that they took a commission off advice he gave to other clubs, so it was in their interests to get MacKenzie as much extra work as they could find. His redesigns at Kingston Heath and Royal Adelaide would be testament enough to his skills, but they went far beyond that, and to many clubs and courses. Yet he was not in Australia for long enough to see through any of his redesigns. He had to rely on those on the ground to implement his schemes.

Amazingly, in his few days at Royal Melbourne, MacKenzie won over the support of Alex Russell, the Australian Amateur Champion of 1924, and Mick Morcom, the greenkeeper at Royal Melbourne. Both soon embraced MacKenzie's principles of golf design.

Southern hemisphere's finest test

MacKenzie redesigned the West Course at Royal Melbourne. Russell and Morcombe reworked the East Course and it is from these two that the Composite Course is drawn for tournament play. The reason for having a composite course is simple: to keep play within the boundaries of a club on which both courses normally cross roads. To provide a grandstand finish, the order of play of the Composite Course has also been changed in recent years, providing a run in of seven par 4s, only one of which is under 400 yards (366m) in length.

New technology and the athleticism of players threaten to destroy even Royal Melbourne. US Open champion, Michael Campbell, played Royal Melbourne in 1996, came back in 2002 and reckoned that each hole played about two clubs shorter. Yet most of the great golfers recognize the individuality of Royal Melbourne. Nick Faldo, for instance, spent hours in 2002 videoing each bunker simply to hope to learn from the experience as a budding architect.

Classic dogleg

The hole that most architects would like to have designed above all others is the 4th on the Composite Course, the 6th on the West, one of MacKenzie's suggestions. It is a simple dogleg, with bunkers in the angle of the dogleg and further bunkers threatening the green. But it is not as simple as that. What really makes the hole is the way it is drawn out of the natural landforms. MacKenzie's bunkering and green offset might seem typical but their execution is inspirational. That is the difference between a good course and a great one.

RIGHT The par-3 5th on the West Course, which plays as the 3rd on the Composite Course, is a superb short hole fortified by bunkers with a fast green that slopes from front to back.

RIGHT The view from behind the green on the par-4 2nd hole on the East Course, approached from left of picture, with Mackenzie's classic dogleg, the 6th on the West Course, stretching into the distance.

CARD OF THE COMPOSITE COURSE

Hole		Distance (yards)	Par
❶	3rd West	354	4
❷	4th West	498	5
❸	5th West	176	3
❹	6th West	450	4
❺	1st East	332	4
❻	2nd East	439	4
❼	3rd East	382	4
❽	4th East	201	3
❾	17th East	557	5
❿	2nd West	483	5
⓫	7th West	147	3
⓬	10th West	304	4
⓭	11th West	454	4
⓮	12th West	464	4
⓯	17th West	438	4
⓰	18th West	432	4
⓱	1st West	428	4
⓲	18th East	442	4
Out		3,389	36
In		3,592	36
Total		6,981	72

BANFF SPRINGS
STANLEY THOMSON 18, FAIRMONT BANFF SPRINGS, BANFF, ALBERTA, CANADA

Stanley Thomson built many of Canada's finest courses and Banff can only be described as world class. At Banff, Thomson had the advantage of working for the Canadian Pacific Railway, who wanted the existing course at their enormous hotel there turned into something worthy of such a luxurious establishment. The advantage of having the railway involved was that transporting large quantities of earth was a simple and relatively inexpensive operation, and Thomson was a master craftsman moulding earth into imaginative golf courses.

Grand gestures in a grand setting

Banff Springs is in the heart of the towering Canadian Rockies and the site selected lay beside two mountain rivers, the Bow and the Spray. Nothing other than grand gestures would suffice to make the course stand out against such an overpowering background. Thomson did not attempt to match the mountain scenery, but he developed a technique he had already used at Jasper Park (which, incidentally, was built for the rival Canadian National Railway) which mirrored and imitated features. So the mounding around a green might be a mirror image of the mountain skyline beyond or he might use water to reflect the background, and so on. It was his sense of proportion and scale which made him such an artist in dirt!

His course, which opened in 1927, began with a terrifying drive across the Spray River from an elevated tee under the shadow of the 770-room hotel. However, in 1992 the Canadian golf architect, Bill Robinson, was called in to build another 9-hole course on land adjacent to Thomson's course. Robinson did not touch Thomson's masterpiece but a new clubhouse was built to serve both courses and

Hole	Distance (yards)	Par
1	432	4
2	179	3
3	536	5
4	199	3
5	431	4
6	381	4
7	610	5
8	158	3
9	510	5
10	225	3
11	424	4
12	449	4
13	232	3
14	447	4
15	480	4
16	421	4
17	384	4
18	585	5
Out	3,436	36
In	3,647	35
Total	7,083	71

CARD OF THE COURSE

Thomson's course now starts at what used to be the 5th hole. It might be said that this hardly matters, but rhythm is an important part of a golf course routing and now that terrifying drive comes at the 15th, by which time the golfer has had plenty of time to get his swing working properly.

Devil's Cauldron

The most famous hole at Banff is the short 4th, once played as the 8th. It has the name Devil's Cauldron and is played from a high tee down over a lake to a tiny green surrounded by expansive bunkers. Mount Rundle makes a stunning backdrop with its rocky cliffs and tree-clad lower slopes.

The season at Banff is short, but while the course is open it has a very Scottish feel, except that elk roam the course at will where red deer might at its Scottish namesake. As built, the course grew to a climax in a sequence of holes alongside the Bow River and these are now played as the 8th to the 14th — superb holes with brilliant (but not excessive) use made of the threat of water, thought-provoking bunkering and a delicious marriage between the design of the golf course and the imposing scenery all around. This is what golf course architecture is all about.

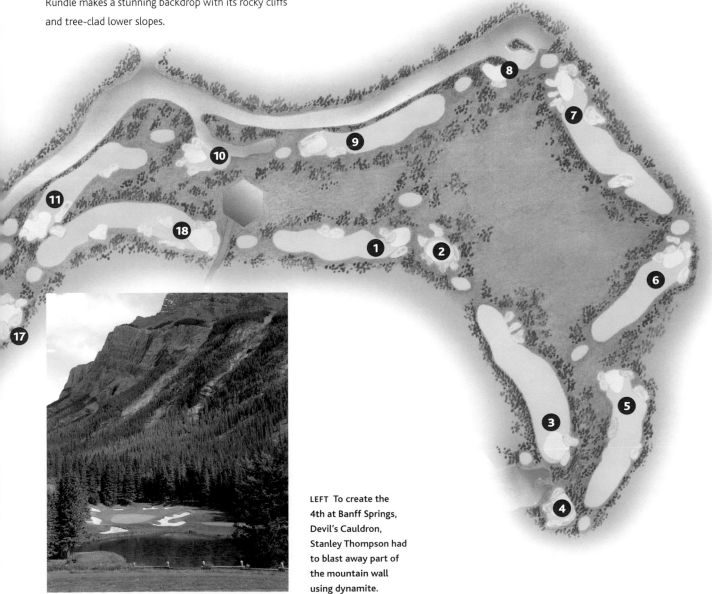

LEFT To create the 4th at Banff Springs, Devil's Cauldron, Stanley Thompson had to blast away part of the mountain wall using dynamite.

INDEX